Jonathan Scott, MBA

Fundamentals of Leisure Business Success
A Manager's Guide to Achieving Success in the Leisure and Recreation Industry

Pre-publication REVIEWS, COMMENTARIES, EVALUATIONS . . .

"**A** fascinating and interesting read (and this is a business book!). Jonathan Scott not only explains contemporary fundamentals of successful business operations, he explains them in a context that demonstrates what most of us within the leisure industry will have to face either every day or at certain points throughout our careers . . . all the situations and work realities you don't learn about in college.

The major case study used is an excellent example of the extremes that can (and do) happen at any recreation-oriented business. All the sections, the style, and the examples shown throughout the book help demystify academic business jargon and unabashedly show the simplicity behind most of it."

Michael Holman
*PGA Professional and Manager,
Trio Ranch Country Club
Golf Operations,
Jeddah, Saudi Arabia*

"**J**onathan Scott uses a case study model to introduce topics of universal applicability in the recreation and leisure market encountered by the professional. The section on 'Building the Commitment to Change,' for instance, applies equally well to the experience in Saudi Arabia as it would to a director taking over an operation in a Florida resort. Unlike a dry textbook, *Fundamentals of Leisure Business Success* teaches theory by demonstrating it in real life practical application. The results of applying management theory are clearly detailed.

Beyond the case study are practical discussions of the common elements or components in the work of a commercial recreation professional. The chapter on pricing is a particularly important discussion and very well done. New and experienced professionals would do well to review this material. Overall, Scott has presented our industry with a very practical and readable blend of theory and practice in the business of leisure. I recommend this book as part of every practitioner's professional library."

Frank Oliveto
Executive Director,
Resort & Commercial
Recreation Association,
Tarpon Springs, FL

"**E**very so often a book comes along that is an absolute must for professional business people. Jonathan Scott's book fits into that category."

Robert Paton
Executive Director,
UK Fitness Industry Association,
Camberley, Surrey,
United Kingdom

"**T**his is the first practitioner-oriented business book I have seen truly designed for professionals working within all aspects of the highly diverse and fragmented leisure industry. The book's many strengths include its style and design, which are not prescriptive, but instead challenge readers to think about and adapt the concepts discussed around their own unique leisure business workplace. It is simply full of ideas, strategies, theories, and applications that have proven to facilitate success in leisure business world-wide and are all too often easily forgotten in the pressures of our everyday work environments. It is a must for everyone who works in leisure and recreation."

Wayne Hasson
President, Aggressors
International Ltd.,
Grand Cayman,
British West Indies

Fundamentals of Leisure Business Success

*A Manager's Guide to Achieving
Success in the Leisure
and Recreation Industry*

HAWORTH Marketing Resources
Innovations in Practice & Professional Services
William J. Winston, Senior Editor

New, Recent, and Forthcoming Titles:

Strategic Planning for Not-for-Profit Organizations by R. Henry Migliore, Robert E. Stevens, and David L. Loudon

Marketing Planning in a Total Quality Environment by Robert E. Linneman and John L. Stanton, Jr.

Managing Sales Professionals: The Reality of Profitability by Joseph P. Vaccaro

Squeezing a New Service into a Crowded Market by Dennis J. Cahill

Publicity for Mental Health Clinicians: Using TV, Radio, and Print Media to Enhance Your Public Image by Douglas H. Ruben

Managing a Public Relations Firm for Growth and Profit by A. C. Croft

Utilizing the Strategic Marketing Organization: The Modernization of the Marketing Mindset by Joseph P. Stanco

Internal Marketing: Your Company's Next Stage of Growth by Dennis J. Cahill

The Clinician's Guide to Managed Behavioral Care by Norman Winegar

Marketing Health Care into the Twenty-First Century: The Changing Dynamic by Alan K. Vitberg

Fundamentals of Strategic Planning for Health-Care Organizations edited by Stan Williamson, Robert Stevens, David Loudon, and R. Henry Migliore

Risky Business: Managing Violence in the Workplace by Lynne Falkin McClure

Predicting Successful Hospital Mergers and Acquisitions: A Financial and Marketing Analytical Tool by David P. Angrisani and Robert L. Goldman

Marketing Research That Pays Off: Case Histories of Marketing Research Leading to Success in the Marketplace edited by Larry Percy

How Consumers Pick a Hotel: Strategic Segmentation and Target Marketing by Dennis Cahill

Applying Telecommunications and Technology from a Global Business Perspective by Jay Zajas and Olive Church

Strategic Planning for Private Higher Education by Carle M. Hunt, Kenneth W. Oosting, Robert Stevens, David Loudon, and R. Henry Migliore

Writing for Money in Mental Health by Douglas H. Ruben

The New Business Values for Success in the Twenty-First Century: Improvement, Innovation, Inclusion, Incentives, Information by John Persico and Patricia Rouner Morris

Marketing Planning Guide, Second Edition by Robert E. Stevens, David L. Loudon, Bruce Wrenn, and William E. Warren

Contemporary Sales Force Management by Tony Carter

4 × 4 Leadership and the Purpose of the Firm by H. H. Pete Bradshaw

Lessons in Leisure Business Success: The Recreation Professional's Business Transformation Primer by Jonathan T. Scott

Guidebook to Managed Care and Practice Management Terminology by Norman Winegar and Michelle L. Hayter

Medical Group Management in Turbulent Times: How Physician Leadership Can Optimize Health Plan, Hospital, and Medical Group Performance by Paul A. Sommers

Defining Your Market: Winning Strategies for High-Tech, Industrial, and Service Firms by Art Weinstein

Defective Bosses: Working for the Dysfunctional Dozen by Kerry Carson and Paula Phillips Carson

Fundamentals of Leisure Business Success

A Manager's Guide to Achieving Success in the Leisure and Recreation Industry

Jonathan Scott, MBA

The Haworth Press
New York • London

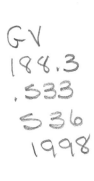

Cover design by Marylouise E. Doyle.

Library of Congress Cataloging-in-Publication Data

Scott, Jonathan (Jonathan T.)
Fundamentals of leisure business success : a manager's guide to achieving success in the leisure and recreation industry / Jonathan Scott.
p.   cm.
Includes bibliographical references and index.
ISBN 0-7890-0445-3 (alk. paper)
1. Leisure industry—Saudi Arabia—Riyadh—Case studies. 2. Leisure industry—Saudi Arabia—Riyadh—Management—Case studies. I. Title.
GV188.3.S33S36 1998
790'.06'9—dc21
97-45776
CIP

CONTENTS

Preface ix

PART I: INTRODUCTION

Leisure: The World's Largest Industry 3

Leisure as Business 7

The Case Study Introduction 11

PART II: THEORIES AND APPLICATIONS

Introduction 31

Building the Commitment to Change 33

Strategy 37

Structure 45

Systems 49

Staff 55

Style 59

Shared Values 65

Skills 71

Change in Retrospect 83

Results 89

Case Study Conclusions 95

Recreation Services Today 99

PART III: COMPONENTS

Introduction   103

Understanding Good Customer (or Guest) Service   105

Difficult Customers   109

Getting the Most from Employees   115

Teamwork and Delegation   121

Volunteers   125

Finance and Accountants   131

The Importance of Marketing   137

Pricing and How to Make It Work Best for You   149

Ethics and Quality   157

Planning Projects, Events, and Activities   163

PART IV: PATHS AND DIRECTIONS

Where to Go for Further Information   171

Conclusion   177

Bibliography   179

Index   183

ABOUT THE AUTHOR

Jonathan T. Scott, MBA, has twenty years of experience in the leisure and recreation industry, having worked in a variety of leisure businesses in five different countries. After years of laboring in, and observing the workings of, these and other leisure businesses, he began to formulate the elements of that which makes leisure businesses successful. Since obtaining his first management position, he has successfully transformed or improved every leisure business to which he has been put in control. Recently, he turned around yet a third leisure business after six years of its insolvency. This business has a large, nationally recognized equestrian operation, numerous tennis and athletic facilities, and the region's first grass golf course.

Preface

Management: The act or art of control. The judicious use of means to accomplish an end. (*Merriam-Webster Dictionary*)

Transformation: To change in structure, appearance, or character. (*Merriam-Webster Dictionary*)

Success. The word implies forward movement and achievement. Being able to manage change is the key to moving ahead. This applies whether change involves an individual or a group of people. Virtually everything done in our private and working lives depends on group or self-management. The same principles that apply to leading organizations are relevant to ourselves by translating into how we, as individuals, make decisions, prioritize, organize, get along with others, plan ahead, and choose to behave. Learning from management techniques also provides us a better understanding of how others think and act the way they do. It also prepares us for our own growth and development and that of the business organizations in which we work.

One of the more interesting ways of learning about change is through the trials and tribulations of others. It is easier and safer to hear about how others faced situations and to gather the information and learn from their experiences than it is to suffer through them yourself. Whether it is true that we learn more from negative experiences is debatable, but I would rather hear of somebody else's mistake before I make a similar one. Hindsight (no matter whose) is a wonderful thing, and it is extremely helpful when one uses it to examine past mistakes and successes. It enables us to imagine different conclusions, opens our minds to other possibilities, and pushes us to be more creative—always with less effort, and bruises, on our part.

The collection of writing presented in this book is done in four separate and distinct parts. Part I examines the scope and substance of the leisure industry and introduces the reader to the importance of business concepts. Part II shows the workings and theories of modern organizational structures through the use of a case study. More important, it examines the concepts of transformation and change. Transformation and change are essential in business *and* personal growth. The study chosen tells the story of the partial transformation of a foreign leisure business. (The word partial is used because transformation is never complete: it is ongoing.) This rather unique business contains many of the diverse operations that the leisure industry encompasses, including children's programs, all types of international sports, competitions, aquatics, arts and crafts, a theater, outside contracts and vendors, community presentations, equipment rentals, local tours and international travel, indoor and outdoor racquet courts, festivals, game rooms, fitness facilities and programs, exhibits, dinner parties, and a host of other services scattered throughout a city of 2.5 million inhabitants. During its two-year "transformation," it went from being considered "not good" to what was commented on as "the best (of its kind) in the country." It was a remarkable journey, one that I began, and one that required the talents and expertise of numerous individuals. It also occurred under circumstances that should have prohibited its success.

The business discussed is located in Riyadh, Saudi Arabia, easily one of the more religiously conservative cities in Saudi. The restrictions and practices mentioned are not typical of that part of the world, or indeed in most of Saudi itself. In many instances, it is a story of extremes. People tend to think and express themselves in extremes. How many times throughout childhood did you hear your mother say something to the effect of, "Put that down before you put your eye out"? When two individuals (or groups) at work or at home are involved in an emotional dispute, listen for the words, "you *always* . . ." or "*every* time . . ." or "you *never* . . ." when, of course, the fact is that "always," "every," and "never" are rarely the case. They are merely exaggerations. Extremes are used because they help us to get our point across (and tend to infuriate the accused).

This time, however, those extremes are genuine. The facts are fascinating and at times unbelievable, but they are true and accurate. *The point is that if this business succeeded and improved under the extreme conditions that will be examined, then almost any busi-*

ness can succeed using the same principles of common sense, determination, and effective business practices. To present the story and the total picture as smoothly as possible, there is a short section, preceding the case study, that explains the business's environment and difficulties by giving a brief history of the country and the business itself before transformation. It deviates from the central theme, but it is essential for better understanding along the format chosen. Please remember that the differences presented are not the central theme of the case study. The main idea is that every country, region, or city has laws, cultural restrictions, and practices regarding what is acceptable and what is not. These *will* affect the leisure business.

The case study is divided into seven categories devised by Richard Pascale, author of *Managing on the Edge*, Anthony Athos of the Harvard Business School, Robert Watermen of McKinsey and Company, and Tom Peters, author of *In Search of Excellence*. The categories are: *Strategy, Structure, Systems, Staff, Style, Shared Values,* and *Skills*. Using these categories allows for a logical look at organizations and what makes them "tick." As this book is not designed to be prescriptive, these categories were also used to create an atmosphere conducive to further thought and reflection, particularly when it comes to your place of employment. No matter what the specialization into which your leisure business falls, it is hoped that the information contained in this book will be found inspiring and useful, and perhaps it can be adapted to promote further success in your own organization. While reading, actively think about how these theories and applications can enrich your working life and the lives of your colleagues. Think about what is needed for you to bring about successful *changes*. Most important, do not be afraid to take action. *Understanding, beginning, and following through* with the *change* process is a recurring theme while making improvements.

In Part III, a different course of action is taken. This eclectic section is a compilation of separate essays written to further discuss the integral areas that are highly relevant to businesses operating in the leisure industry. The topics (many contain smaller case study examples) deal with common sense and the often basic knowledge that we all need reminding of from time to time. These themes, touched upon in the case study, are examined with more depth. They also comprise much of what is discussed in business schools today to bring about business and personal improvements. Hopefully some of the subject matter, thoughts, and information presented may appear new or be shown in a different perspective and will therefore prove to be thought-provoking.

Finally, Part IV provides information needed to continue the search for additional knowledge about the leisure industry, the leisure profession, business, or transformation, and how to get more involved. There is simply so much information about the leisure industry or business available that it is sometimes difficult to figure out where and how to get started in order to begin a search. This section should help to point readers in the right direction.

I would like to express my gratitude to many people who helped with the encouragement and guidance necessary to complete this book. Special thanks are due to Mr. John Threlfall of London Guildhall University for his tutorage with the original thesis. Mr. David Bird, Mr. David Hunt, Dr. Owen Tamby, Mr. Ramnarian Dhanipersad, Mr. John Lynch, Ms. Imelda (Johanna) O'Donnell, and Mr. Najeeb Quasrani, all on the faculty of Western International University in London, are due thanks for providing countless hours of instruction and assistance as I earned my MBA at that same university. My uncle, Dr. Robert F. Steidel, (retired from a Chairmanship at the University of California, Berkeley) was enormously helpful by providing his skills as an experienced editor. It would be impossible to put into words how much I owe these people.

My parents, George and Audrey Scott, have also been extremely helpful—especially my father, who, after thanking me for buying his first computer, sat quietly watching while I "borrowed" it from him in order to write this book. Finally, it would be terribly remiss to not acknowledge the entire staff of Recreation Services for their hard work and dedication, including Catherine Chamberlain, Rommel Rint, Randy Vilan, Gapur Sahibil, Fattah Suliman Ibraham, and the others. The staff of this leisure business were the ones who made the success, examined in the case study, possible. It was this success that helped inspire the writing of this book.

PART I:
INTRODUCTION

Leisure:
The World's Largest Industry

Industry: A distinctive group of productive enterprises. (*Merriam-Webster Dictionary*)

Profession: A calling requiring specialized knowledge and academic preparation. The whole body of persons engaged in a calling. (*Merriam-Webster Dictionary*)

Having fun often comes at a price, and the revenues collected from having fun are staggering. Worldwide statistics for travel and tourism alone, just one slice of the leisure industry, added up to over three trillion dollars in 1994 and it has been estimated that one in sixteen people worldwide are employed in this expanding leisure-oriented field. According to the Institute of Leisure and Amenity Management in Berkshire, England, leisure represents almost 20 percent of gross national product (GNP), amounting to $1 trillion in Great Britain, and employs roughly 14 percent of the working population. In the United States, some estimates claim that up to and over $800 billion (or roughly 15 percent of the U.S. GNP of $6 trillion) is spent annually toward leisure pursuits, and the numbers continue to grow. According to Stynes (1995), approximately $40,000 in consumer spending generates a full-time job. A trillion dollars in leisure spending would then account for about one-quarter of all jobs within the United States in 1990. Also, because every job in leisure generates another job in a supporting industry, it can be assumed that nearly half of all American jobs are linked to the leisure industry. But how accurate are these numbers? Explaining the leisure industry's economic figures is difficult, as they are often written and displayed with a variety of formats because of the leisure industry's enormous scope. For example, hotels are considered a part of leisure, and yet the components that enable these businesses to function (e.g., laundry, dry cleaning, furniture, uniforms, raw materials, etc., all playing a part in the industry) are not always entered into the whole equation. Where does one draw the line? Since it becomes a matter of interpretation, there is a wide divergence of a total number of leisure expenditure figures although the numbers depicted are always enormous.

Leisure is a relatively new industry. Until man had enough time to actively pursue recreational interests, leisure activity was almost exclusively restricted to royalty, the rich, or the aristocracy. Leisure, and its industry, became a byproduct of the postmodern industrial revolution, and it has since grown, and continues to grow, at an incredible rate. "The leisure industry is one of the fastest growing in the world today" (Joseph and Ritchie, 1990). "Current theory predicts that the size of the leisure market is going to rapidly increase over the next few decades" (*Administration of Leisure and Recreation Services,* 1992). Because leisure now plays such a major role in almost every aspect and class of society, leisure activities involve themselves in the lives of virtually all of us. With these activities ranging from athletic events to zoo visits, it would be quite impossible to describe the complete scope of opportunities and interests available during leisure time. Many businesses, sciences, hobbies, and other seemingly unrelated areas can fall under the industry's umbrella. These include, but are not limited to: museums, parks, libraries, entertainment (television, music, cinema, etc.), the arts (opera, ballet, theater, etc.), travel and tourism, clubs, the sciences (on an amateur level), community programs, and scholastic courses.

Of course, there are the more traditional leisure-based activities. Athletics (amateur and professional), crafts and hobbies, amusement parks, resorts, discos, sailing and boating, community centers, social clubs and activities, and a continuing list of programs and activities are all individually or socially based around having fun or occupying spare time. *In fact, what is done or pursued during time spent away from work or duties makes up the broad definition of leisure.* Almost any activity can be classified under leisure if the right attitude of mind is adopted toward it. Even reading or going to a restaurant can be described as leisure activities. A university professor once told me that it is virtually impossible to establish a definition for recreation and leisure. Any attempt founders on what any one individual sees as recreational.

Traditional industries have firmly entrenched themselves within the leisure field. The area of retail sales is a good example. Clothing, foodstuffs, apparatus, and equipment that focus on leisure activities are sold at many leisure facilities. Leaders of fund-raisers, charity drives, education, and technology often use a leisure-based format as a vehicle to accomplish their goals. The virtual elasticity of the industry in the public and private sectors, both profit and nonprofit, includes:

- central, local, and federal governments,
- industrial and commercial companies and corporations,
- educational institutions,
- public bodies,
- the military,
- professional organizations, and
- voluntary organizations.

The sheer number of leisure locations, opportunities, offerings, choices, and amounts of money are enormous. Take a look at the high salaries demanded by, and given to, musical artists, entertainment stars, and athletes. Society reserves its highest pay for those who structure our leisure time. With all that leisure involves, the people employed and the revenue generated, it is understandable why government has a keen interest in the field. Politics and economics have an important effect on the leisure industry and vice versa. Government and politics have controlled and manipulated leisure to meet the interests of state and local authorities and those they serve (Wilson, 1988). Think of the Olympics and the amount of pride, attention, and business this spectacle brings to its host city.

The word "leisure" came into the English language from the Latin "licere," meaning to be allowed. "License" comes from the same root. The implications suggest permission, lawfulness, and morality (ibid). Yet these are not the only affectations. Leisure reflects on culture, identity, and nationalism, and it can be the source of much focus and pride. The significance of these implications and the influences they have on differing outlooks on leisure, the types of activities that are declared suitable, and the time and place they are deemed to be appropriate can be astounding. Again, think of the Olympics as an example and its development over the years in regard to women and their participation, style of dress, and popularity.

But, let's not lose our focus. Leisure is big business. It has also become a profession. As such, it needs to follow the principles of education, honesty, productivity, profitability, fairness, competitiveness, responsibility, and success that we expect from any business or profession. (However, in leisure's case, a little fun should be thrown in as well!) By its very nature as an industry, leisure requires planning and management. Times and locations need to be determined. Clients wish to be formally instructed and challenged; marketing techniques must be examined and used; equipment must be purchased and stored; safety and employment responsibilities must be met. A wide scope of issues and concerns needs to be addressed in order for leisure pursuits to be administered safely, efficiently, profitably (not just in monetary terms), and effectively.

Organizing leisure presents a particular set of problems that are, to a large extent, a result of the varied content and unique nature of the product itself. Too often, activities fail because not enough time and thought has been given to their planning. Good management skills in particular are demanded because the leisure industry is people-based, and more often than not, managers get things done through the efforts of other people. The management problem facing all organizers is that they cannot depend on an established routine in which a prescribed set of actions will produce or ensure a successful program. There is nothing like a poorly run operation, and the bad feelings and adverse publicity it creates, to ruin planned events or activities. However, a well-organized and successful program can bring considerable benefits to its organizers by promoting a positive and professional image and inspiring participants to come back for more (*Administration of Leisure and Recreation Services,* 1992). Numerous dynamic changes in trends, technology, and fickle interests provide endless circumstances to test teamwork, management, and leadership skills. These are the challenging concepts on which healthy leisure businesses rely.

Leisure as Business

Business: . . . purposeful activity . . . a role or function . . . an immediate task or objective. . . . commercial or mercantile activity engaged in as a means of livelihood . . . a commercial or sometimes an industrial enterprise . . . personal concern . . . serious activity requiring time and effort. . . . (*Webster's Collegiate Dictionary*)

A popular definition of management states that management is the effective and efficient utilization of money, manpower, and materials. Experience broadens this "utilization of" to really mean lack of funds, debtors who refuse to (or cannot) pay, audits, poor record keeping (i.e., money problems); tempers, egos, apathy, arrogance, misinformed/untrained/inexperienced/missing employees, employees running late or schedules shot-to-hell (i.e., manpower problems); broken equipment, stolen equipment, overpriced equipment, lack of equipment (i.e., material problems); and similar business realities. A good business knows that these unfortunate realities have solutions and continuously seeks these solutions out. Satisfaction is derived from the successful handling of problems and the preparedness of being able to deal with any new ones. "Profits" that are obtained could translate into financial gains and/or self-satisfaction or social-satisfaction.

While I was in business school, one of the university professors began his class by talking about profits. He suggested that whenever the term "business" is used, images are conjured up of greedy, back-stabbing, overly ambitious individuals striving toward creating nothing more than a pile of money into which they can stick their filthy hands. His point was that there is sometimes a general misconception that business concerns itself only with profits, whatever the cost. Perhaps in some instances this may be the case, but for most of the world it is not. Profits are generally used to establish growth and meet the unending array of life's problems and chal-

7

lenges that jeopardize business security and the jobs that go with it. Business is not about the popular soap opera representation of revenge and power play. Business is about livelihoods, competition, and survival.

Whatever the business venture, every enterprise has the need to pursue smooth and efficient operations. This means the development, implementation, and selling of a product or service as ethically, cost-effectively, and problem-free as possible. The final result must be of high enough standard to attract customers. Participation by paying customers is pursued in order to provide the sales (or involvement) that lead to wage and job stability. Investigating the subject of business takes into consideration the roles and functions that are required to complete the process of providing a product or service successfully. Leisure business is no exception. Whether it is to provide an activity for a group of children, organized overseas travel, or a sports competition, the many different facets of leisure demand that costs, schedules, labor, materials, and activity processes are administered in such a way that they attract and satisfy the customer or participant competitively. To have all of this done efficiently and expeditiously is the aim of business operations. Again, the aims of leisure businesses are no exception.

Leisure businesses come in all shapes and sizes, and they employ a wide number and variety of people. Whether objectives are geared toward nonprofit concerns or the making of a profit, good solid business practices should always be followed. Materials and time cost money, in one way or another, and keeping an eye on the "bottom line" is essential. Large sections of bookstores and libraries have been organized, selling or distributing a proliferation of written material designed to instruct readers in the "proper" way to implement these practices. Yet, with every business and industry being different and unique, it is impossible to cover every aspect of successful business operations and claim tailor-made survival plans. That is accomplished by an educated workforce who can turn basic ideas and knowledge into workable solutions they can call their own. Every leisure employee should learn basic business and organizational principles because information is power. An increase in power means that more control can be taken in the leisure professional's life.

It might be difficult to try to imagine running an arts and crafts festival the same as the operations of General Motors, but there are similarities. Both involve skilled and knowledgeable people who need motivation, direction, organization, coordination, and a common pursuit. Both need costs and expenses to remain low while establishing an organizational framework where quality remains high.

While there are similarities, there are of course a number of differences. Despite the vast array of popular management and business books, many books seem to focus primarily on the larger, more familiar corporations—the ones with popular brand names, millions of dollars of capital, and thousands of employees. Few of these books address the service profession, and fewer still discuss leisure, the world's largest industry. There is also a tendency by those of us in the industry to, for the most part, ignore the highly relevant information that is available regarding successful business operations and teachings. Instead, we concentrate on program idea and creation.

Perhaps there is the impression that business information is dull or boring and does not pertain to the leisure profession. If so, this could not be further from the truth. A successful business is, in essence, the fruition of an idea or set of goals. It reflects the style and character of its creators. Management (including self-management), through a process of purposeful direction, encourages and directs the development and use of talents and abilities by productively following through with ideas and goals. It is not always fun and games, and it does require hard work, but in the end, what is created represents the effort invested. We alone determine how our organizations will run. Only when greed, apathy, or the blandness of uniformity entrench themselves within a business do misconceptions come into view. Modern business is realizing that productivity is the result of a happy and contented workforce pulsating with innovation and employee input. These are the lessons being taught today at seminars and business schools around the world. More important, these are the ideas being used to *transform* a number of businesses. Viewing your leisure operation as a business does not take away any of its fun, character, or flavor. Instead, it can open the door to a whole world of possibilities full of style, innovation, and flair.

The Case Study Introduction

Every country imposes its own customs, morals, restrictions, and legalities, which are reflected in the leisure pursuits of its people. The purpose of this case study is not to make judgments as to what is right and what is wrong. The message is of transformational change and how it can be implemented within leisure businesses even under rather severe limitations. Creative thinking and initiative are powerful tools in adapting leisure business to a more successful level. Saudi Arabia is used as an example because the differences that myself and the staff both presented and had to deal with in our leisure business provide some excellent examples of instigating change in an environment that had prohibited others from succeeding. Every business must face similar obstacles at one point or another, perhaps not in the extremes presented here, but certainly in a variety of other ways.

While reading the case study, think about any similarities you have experienced or encountered regarding leisure businesses—NOT THE DIFFERENCES. As with any business or region, a better understanding of some basic history, practices, and organizational setups helps to answer many questions as to why things are as they are and how they can be changed for the better. It would be difficult to discuss the case study presented in these pages without a similar presentation of Saudi Arabia.

The foundation of modern Saudi Arabia began in 1902 with the capture of the city of Riyadh by Abdul Azziz Bin Saud, from whom the country takes its name. The consolidation of a diverse and independent people was much more difficult than the conquest. Within a few decades, Abdul Azziz managed to unify the numerous and often feuding tribes that regulated the majority of what now makes up the country's regions. This was accomplished through intermarriages, battles, and a strict interpretation of the Islamic religion.

Wahhibism is the name given to the rigid religious interpretation of Islam to which the Saudi people adhere. Mohammad Ibn Abdul Wahhab, the founder of Wahhibism, was born in the early eighteenth century and chose to dedicate his life to studying the Koran and interpreting its words in the most strict and literal way (Lacey, 1981). Islam at the time was practiced in a very liberal and sectarian manner. Abdul sought to do away with this through, among other things, the apparent elimination of levity.

It was the Al-Saud family, the ancestors of Abul Azziz, who welcomed Abdul Wahhab into their fold, and an alliance was struck. Wahhab soon reformed them to his ways: dancing, smoking, and music were forbidden, as were shrines and any luxury, lest they detract from worshipping the true God (ibid). Reforms were just the beginning. The teacher also preached conversion and that it was the duty of all good Muslims to purify those around them. If persuasion did not work, then stronger methods were justified (ibid). This religious fervor was of great use many years later when Abdul Azziz took over the country, for it was not only his family's considered right to rule that inspired the young man, but also the call to a Holy War and its cleansing of the country, cities, and peoples of immorality.

In the 1930s, oil was discovered, and with the find came an unending flood of Western governments and companies anxious to capitalize on the country's reserves. Changes occurred very rapidly. Although it may be difficult to comprehend today, fifty years ago, Riyadh was a small, Middle Eastern, Arab community built of little more than sticks and mud. It was encircled by a mud brick wall containing five gates that opened at sunrise and closed at sunset. In a fifty-year period, it has become a sprawling metropolis of 2.5 million inhabitants. The skyline is littered with the most modern steel and glass buildings. Multilane motorways, microwave towers, brand-name department and food stores, shopping malls, and high-tech gadgets are in abundance. Indeed, changes have occurred so fast that conflicts have arisen by the hundreds. Many Saudis feel they are losing a grip on their culture. Oil has brought riches these former desert wanderers could never have conceived. Unfortunately, it has also brought more than its share of problems.

When radio was first introduced into the Kingdom, it was viewed by the religious conservatives as an instrument of Satan and an evil tool of the infidel West. Eventually it was accepted, but only after King Abdul Azziz quietly ordered the construction of radio towers that, in the beginning, were only allowed to broadcast readings from the Koran. And so it continues today as new technological advancements, ideas, and the Western methods often required to implement them are introduced. Saudi Arabia continues to face a huge dilemma. It desperately wants to be modernized (not Westernized), "but it needs Western technology to get the economy moving and fulfill a dream of self-reliance. Inevitably Saudi Arabia has a love-hate relationship with the West" (Hobday, 1979). Because of a need for technology and a low opinion of labor, Saudi Arabia relies heavily on foreign workers. It is estimated that, at this writing, over one-third of the country's population consists of foreigners. Most come from developing world countries and are exploited as cheap labor. However, a sizable number come from the West.

Because most Saudis feel that their country's natural deposits of oil are a gift of Allah, popular opinion also suggests that the wealth this oil creates means the Saudi people are meant to be served. Along with this belief comes the feeling of inherent leadership. Saudis enjoy being at the top, and a lack of understanding exists that some semblance of experience or knowledge is required to get there. "Everyone wants to start at the top, and almost all, especially those with some education, expect white-collar work in an office, regardless of whether or not they are appropriately trained for it" (McGregor and Nydell, 1981). Naturally, because of the country's rapid transformation, there was a shortage of educated and experienced Saudis to take over all its operations. The lack of any extensive formal education system dictated that, previously, many Saudis would have to go overseas for their education, much to the chagrin of the religious conservatives. Outsiders with specialized education and experience-based skills are in great demand to counterbalance these effects.

With so many individuals from so many different countries (there were over forty-two cultures represented in my last workplace alone) providing much of the modernization and infrastructure of Saudi Arabia, it is not surprising that there is a feeling from the Saudi people that their culture is being inundated with foreigners. The differences these workers represent are barely tolerated. Whether this is brought about by local resentment or an arrogant West remains difficult to distinguish. Dr. Mujahid Al-Sawwa, an Oxford-educated former professor of Islamic law, speaks for those in the Kingdom who regard themselves as enlightened. "Islam believes in religious tolerance. You just have to practice your religion in private" (Mackey, 1987). Conflict between the Saudi culture and its foreign workforce is an unfortunate certainty. This is particularly true in Riyadh, easily one of the most conservative of Saudi's regions.

Matters are made worse when one takes into consideration that the Saudis have been ripped off by virtually every contractor, company, and salesman they have dealt with from Anchorage to Zanzibar. The misconduct and disrespect for Saudi ways by foreigners does little to ease the situation. A great deal of mistrust lies on both sides. This is the environment that often greets outside workers entering Riyadh for their first time, and it does not deter the flow. A large number of foreign workers experience culture shock and are embittered and angry with the changes they must make. Most simply arrive for the tax-free wages supplemented by heavily subsidized (or free) food, housing, and utilities (McGregor and Nydell, 1981). Generous holiday time is also a bonus.

It is unfortunate that quite a number of those entering the country are unaware of what they must adapt to. It was astonishing to see the number of foreigners arriving in Saudi after selling their homes and cars and removing their children from school, without having undertaken a single bit of research into the country, its people, or its customs. Most of these expatriates are disturbed at what they find. Even Muslims from other countries are surprised at the pervasive fundamentalism and mistrust of foreigners. For example, censorship of foreign publications and all news items is severe. *Time, Newsweek, The Economist, Le Monde,* and other popular publications reach the shops with "offensive" material torn from them and their photographs of women heavily covered in black felt pen (Lacey, 1981). Mail can be opened and searched by authorities. Everything except the mosques must close for prayers—twenty minute or so, five times a day. Passports are taken (for "safekeeping") by employers after entering the country, and exit visas are required to leave.

Another sight seen as offensive by expatriates is the treatment of women. Much has been written about the role of women in a strict Islamic regime. Indeed, apart from keeping a good home and producing and raising children, there seems to be little for them to do. During the 1960s, King Faisal was able to establish women's right to an education, but even today this is limited. Many simple privileges are denied to women. Women are not allowed to drive and are not supposed to venture out by themselves (for their own "protection" and "safekeeping"). Incredibly, women are not allowed to testify in court because by *law* they are:

> more emotional than men and will distort their testimony; not participants in public life, and therefore are not capable of understanding what they observe; completely dominated by men (and men, by the grace of God, are deemed superior), so will only testify as to what the last man told them; forgetful and cannot be considered reliable. (Sasson, 1992)

Today, all females, including foreign workers and wives, are required to wear traditional long black garments that cover their entire bodies. Single females are housed separately, and all females must conform to male dominance in one form or another. Most women cannot travel without their husband's or employer's permission. Strict segregation of the sexes for example, even among small school children, is enforced.

Foreigners in general are not accorded the same rights as Saudis, and this is especially true of non-Muslims. The Saudi police are not famous for their lenient treatment of foreigners, and the conditions for expatriates appear to have deteriorated in recent years under the influence of religious zealots (*The Daily Telegraph*, 1990). Numerous petty restrictions on women that are a part of Islamic law have been extended into the expatriate community in a way that was not previously the case, and single women have been subjected to special rules, imposed by employers, regarding their conduct outside of working hours (ibid). Recreation, which forms almost everything that one does in Saudi Arabia outside working hours, is deeply affected by all of these mandates.

Recreational facilities for foreigners in Riyadh are limited, and boredom, particularly for wives, is a major problem. Islam impinges on virtually all aspects of the foreigners' lives. It regulates the days, governs what is eaten, controls behavior, and determines, to a large extent, recreational activities (Mackey, 1987). Much of the history of the country since 1974 involves the government's attempts to force Westerners to conform to religious dictates and, at the same time, make acceptable concessions to its foreign workforce in order to recruit and hold its technical expertise (ibid).

These concessions are often what made life tolerable to those not willing to adjust to, or embrace, an Islamic lifestyle. *Private recreation programs were a part of these concessions. The advent of leisure and recreation facilities is of exceptional importance in the attraction and retention of an expatriate workforce.* With complete separation of single males and females, even sometimes among married couples (single males and females can be jailed if seen together), and the absence of cinemas, pubs, social facilities, and the like, it is easy to become bored and frustrated. "In the world of Saudi Arabia, any form of public entertainment fell into the category of sin . . . the foreigner often remains on his own to make his entertainment . . . people working at isolated work sites or large companies truly suffer" (Mackey, 1987). Many expatriates escape into the desert or the abundant "underground" social life. However, there is always the threat of being spotted and punished by the Mutowa, the country's religious officials empowered with the task of enforcing Islamic compliance. The Mutowa are a surly and uncompromising group greatly feared by both nationals and foreigners.

Still, life for the compromising foreigner who practices discretion can be rewarding, and it is unfair to concentrate only on the country's negative aspects. Riyadh is unique in the severity of its restrictions. Many other parts of the country are much more forward thinking, particularly the coastal cities, where the populace has been greeting and working with foreigners for thousands of years. Times and conditions are changing rapidly, with the majority of Saudi citizens wanting to modernize, all the while remaining devoted to their religious beliefs. This is the main contention between modern Saudi Arabia and the conservative fundamentalists, who think that all contemporary improvements are wrong. Despite these conflicts, particularly when it comes to leisure pursuits, most large companies do make efforts to provide recreation to their employees, and most compounds where foreigners live are enclosed by high walls and are guarded to ensure privacy. Unpleasant incidents are not a daily occurrence, and Saudi culture is rich, interesting, and very much family based.

It is not the intention of this book to focus on the conflicts Western society has with Saudi tradition. However, when one is providing the service of recreation and leisure that contradicts many basic principles of the host country, it is important to be honest and direct about its implications, environment, and possible problems. Only through the understanding of the Saudi culture and its history and regulations can one begin to appreciate the challenges that managing a leisure business can pose. Facing these situations every day was the primary task. What proved to be most exasperating was the inconsistency with which some "offenses" were considered punishable. We were constantly on our toes.

THE HOSPITAL
(THE CORPORATE CENTER
WHERE THE BUSINESS WAS LOCATED)

The Hospital was established in the early 1970s as a referral medical center and a first-class medical facility for the royal family, government officials, and other important figures. In practice, virtually anyone can be seen at the institution through the benevolence of the Saudi royal family. Because of generous government grants and subsidies, the Hospital is able to order the most modern technological equipment. No expense is spared. For example, as the story goes, a few years ago, Canada could only afford four magnetic resonance imaging machines for its hospitals. Riyadh, alone, had six. Two were at the Hospital. Working with this equipment are some of the best operators and physicians recruited from all over the world. The Hospital has continued to grow over the years and by 1992 could boast 500 beds. A research department complete with the Middle East's first nuclear cyclotron (capable of manufacturing the isotopes needed for X-rays, radiation therapy, and other medical procedures) was added some time ago and is fully operational.

At the last count, over 3,000 people from forty-two different countries were employed by the Hospital, and along with this number, more than 2,000 dependents (spouses and children) were housed on various sites. In Saudi Arabia, it is very common for large businesses and institutions to be, to a large degree, self-sufficient. Most have their own electrical power plants, water treatment works, maintenance departments, complete housing facilities for workers, transportation systems for employees to and from work, recreation departments, restaurants, food stores, and a host of other services provided for the operation of the organization and its major services. This complex setup easily leads to the need for 3,000 employees. The Hospital also has an enormous amount of administrative personnel. Generally, only Saudi nationals can hold the top management positions. Because of the country's planning strategies to have nationals eventually run all businesses as well as the Saudi distaste of menial labor, more and more Saudis are squeezed into administrative appointments before their time. Everything has a sense of hierarchy (Lacey, 1981).

According to Handy's (1993) classification of corporate culture, the Hospital would be visualized as pyramid shaped, with many levels of management dictating reams of paperwork, policies, bureaucracy, and red tape. Indeed, it was mentioned by some employees that the Hospital had more physicians than beds and more administrators than physicians! Vinnicombe (1988) states that "The higher his position in the hierarchy, the more the manager is concerned with strategic matters. . . ." However, at the Hospital, most senior management appeared to spend the majority of their time "refereeing" departmental and employee disputes. Most writers and researchers of business organizations would almost certainly label the Hospital as formal and rigid. Formal organizations are known to have many regulations and procedures, poor communication, high levels of stress and frustration, and low employee morale. A supervisor of the Hospital's laboratories once stated that the administrative functioning of the Hospital contradicted every principle he had learned at different universities concerning good management. This same man, a published researcher, held two master's degrees.

Although the Hospital had a good reputation for medical care, the various departments did not always act as a team. Bickering, fighting over turf, writing nasty memos, and refusing to be cooperative caused many interdepartmental problems. Often there was no coordination with even the largest plans or purchases. One time, in 1994, electrical power at the Hospital was cut off. Two of the generators had failed to function properly because of a lack of proper maintenance. When the backup unit was operated, it served no purpose. The Hospital operated on 110 volts, and the enormously expensive backup machine generated 220 volts. This was only part of a surprising number of mishaps that afflicted the Hospital.

Because Recreation Services was physically and structurally separate from the Hospital, our offices were a key vantage point from which to listen and observe the constant struggle of these departments to perform basic functions. Part of this was due to a top-heavy administration, but I believe that this also came about through the arrogance and conceit of a number of employees who always let it be known that they worked at the Hospital which catered to the country's VIPs. Incredibly, this led to some departments trying to go it alone, without the consent or valuable insight from others deeply affected by changes in policy or procedure.

Others apparently resented the constant influx of new employees after they themselves had worked at the Hospital for many years. It was uncommon for visitors to my office to *not* comment on the unfriendliness of the Hospital staff. After having worked in the recreation field in Riyadh for two years prior to coming to the Hospital, this sometimes hostile environment was quite shocking compared to the camaraderie experienced during that time at another hospital-based leisure business located just across town. Employment in Recreation Services would prove to be a mixed blessing.

THE CLUB AND RECREATION SERVICES

Despite the enormous wealth generated by its oil industry, Saudi Arabia, as a result of growth and waste, has become a debtor nation. Each year the situation grows worse. At the time of this writing for instance, a growing number of suppliers and contractors are refusing to do business with the Hospital until its debts have been paid (Pyle, Hall, and Whitehead, 1995).

Although not as severe, the situation was somewhat similar in the mid 1980s when the idea of the Club "corporation" was formed. The Hospital had been faced with a dilemma. It could no longer afford to put money into recreation services, day care, the beauty and barber shops, and a series of other services that employees had come to expect. Nor did these services have much to do with the basic operations of a hospital. At the same time, there was a genuine understanding that these same services needed to be improved and expanded to maintain employee retention. Several small businesses (gift shops, restaurants, florists, etc.) that were run by outside contractors were located at several sites around the Hospital's grounds. There was a concern that some sort of governing body needed to watch over these operations to ensure that they conformed to certain standards and did not contradict the Hospital's mission.

The solution was to set up a small "corporation" that would function on its own and oversee these various services. These services and contracts would, in theory, be separate business concerns, able to stand on their own. Fees would have to be charged for their use. The Hospital would not financially support these businesses. However, all equipment, materials, and buildings required by the services would be handed over to the "corporation's" management at no cost. Nothing such as this had ever been attempted before; some even questioned its legality. Financially, the Hospital had no other option, as it did not wish to handle any more outside contracts. In 1986, despite much objection to the very principles of the organization, the Club was established. By 1993, it employed fifty-nine people from twelve countries.

The Club is governed by ten "Executive Committee" Board members. These board members are comprised of department heads, hospital directors, and other upper management administrators who, according to the Club's charter, are replaced every three years. The Executive Director of the Hospital's Research Department was named as the Executive Committee Board's Chairman, and he reported directly to the Hospital's Chief Executive Director (named as the Club's President, although he never attended meetings). Day-to-day duties and administration are handled by the Club's "Executive Assistant and Director." (Saudis, as with many others, love titles.) This man was who I reported to directly. In the past, the Head of Recreation (or the "Coordinator"—the title was changed when a Westerner took over) was given a seat on the committee but not a vote. Within three months, I was the first recreation manager to be awarded this privilege despite initial resentment from the Chairman, who sometimes considered me as an outsider. (I had been hired by the Hospital to help tackle the numerous problems the Club had not been able to resolve.) All other employees were hired by the Club.

True to maintaining the style from which it was born, the Club's executive committee members seemed to be quite keen on establishing policies and dictates without any in-depth knowledge or observation of the business's divisions. This is the classic "value destroying" situation induced by many corporate centers, as Richard Koch discusses in *The Financial Times Guide to Strategy* (1995). This is brought about not only from flawed or poorly implemented corporate strategy, but also from the expense of corporate administration, the inexperience of corporate executives pertaining to the running of their divisions, and the fact that centers should often do little more than act as an intermediary between the business and its finances (banking) (Koch, 1995).

The Club received revenue for its operations from a number of different sources. Rents collected from outside vendors holding contracts to run their services at these locations, and service/activity fees from Club operations, were paid directly to the Club. In return, the Club would be expected to continually repair and maintain these buildings and facilities, purchase any additional equipment and supplies, and fully staff the operations with qualified personnel. This would have to be done with no internal or external financial subsidies or grants—an exceptionally rare situation in Saudi Arabia.

Revenue came from several different areas:

- *Membership Fees.* Employees could join the Club and would be given substantial discounts on all its services, including over 200 independent businesses throughout Riyadh (in exchange for advertising in the Club's brochure).
- *Rentals.* Revenue from outside contractors, including: Marriott, Baskin-Robbins, Safeway, and local businesses. (The Club operated at a profit thanks to these rentals. They covered losses in every other area.)
- *Donations.* These were submitted by benevolent local businesses or individuals.

- *Merchandise Sales.* Items sold included neckties, T-shirts, pens, frisbees, etc., with the Club logo.
- *Investments.* Net profits were invested in various stocks or funds.
- *A Pastry Shop.* This shop was established because Saudis are generally fond of sweets.
- *Employee Loans.* Over one million dollars was given to employees as *interest free* loans (adhering to Islamic tradition).

Revenues were also collected from the following divisions under the direct control of the Recreation Coordinator:

- *Barber Shop.* This was a small shop with two barbers.
- *Beauty Shop.* The only other area that consistently generated profits. This shop had three beauticians.
- *Child Care Services.* With fifteen full- and part-time employees, the child care area of the Club consisted of two separate buildings and could handle a total of seventy-two children.
- *Recreation Services.* This is the main focus of the case study that follows.

For many employees and their dependents, Recreation Services comprised a great deal of what was done outside work hours. When the Club idea was conceived, concern was raised regarding having employees pay for that which had, in the past, been provided free of charge. Dissent grew rapidly among Hospital staff. Why did they have to pay for what other companies willingly gave to their employees? Besides, recruiters tell prospective employees that these services are part of work contracts. The conflict was resolved by having employees pay for one-half of the services. *A primary reason for the existence of the Club was to finance and subsidize Recreation Services.* To keep the employees happy, Recreation Services was to remain a money loser, *something I was reminded of repeatedly.* I think part of this came from the belief that any type of profit here was seen as some form of usury—a great offense to Muslims. Unfortunately, this practice had also led to the department's downfall over the years. This "policy" also caused a significant amount of heated discussion among the Club's executive committee board.

Upon arrival at Recreation Services in early February of 1993, I was met by many shocking sights. For over a decade, the department had been subject to apathy, mismanagement, and neglect. Employee morale was exceptionally low. Most were motivated by threats from the administrative offices. Recreation staff had little or no leadership, literally walking around with virtually no sense of direction. Few could answer any questions concerning the department. Most acted independently, trying to make the few programs they offered successful. Some hardly bothered working at all or were illicitly operating their own private services during company time.

In the three years prior to my arrival, not one piece of recreation equipment had been ordered or purchased. When asked how an activity could be run without materials, the reply was that participants were required to bring their own. If people wanted basketball lessons, they would have to bring their own basketball. The same applied for table tennis, arts and crafts—everything! It was impossible to determine to where the department's funds were disappearing.

The facilities fared even worse. Approximately 60 percent of the locations (Recreation Services comprised twelve different locations around Riyadh) were either completely unusable, or were so damaged and filthy that few customers tried to use them. All of the tennis courts had cracks, potholes, and similar damage. Swimming pool areas were disgusting. The surfacing used to protect bathers from the hot sun on the pool decks was caked with filth and, in many cases, was decomposing and in tatters. It was not uncommon for housekeepers to be seen washing dishes or dirty diapers at the pool edge. Human feces were found at some pool locations. Vandalism was rampant and could not be halted.

Safety procedures and equipment were completely forgotten. One of the main reasons for my being hired was the death of a fourteen-year-old girl who drowned at one of the swimming pool locations, in full view of over thirty people who were minding their own business. Few facilities or areas were locked in the evenings, and employees wandered in and out at all hours "borrowing" whatever they wanted. The badges required to be worn by all eligible employees for entrance to the facilities were never checked. The staff were just too afraid to confront the largely unfriendly Hospital workforce.

Squash courts and racquetball courts contained large chunks of peeling paint, water damage, and corroding ceilings and walls. The so-called main exercise room contained one broken-down, twelve-year-old Universal weight machine. All the other apparatus for exercise had actually been constructed by disgruntled Hospital employees out of scrap metal and pipes. Employees had given up asking for anything new, and there simply were not enough facilities for all the Hospital's 5,000 employees and dependents. Indeed, most of the facilities that were available consisted of dirty, unpainted walls, stained carpets, and broken equipment. Some were used primarily for storing broken furniture and other discarded items. At some locations, broken furniture outnumbered the usable pieces.

My first months at the Hospital were met with numerous verbal confrontations, many at shouting level, with frustrated Hospital employees exclaiming what a waste of time Recreation Services was and how all previous managers had been useless and ineffective. I was told I would be the same. If I was not being shouted at, the constant complaints (all valid, mind you) from recreations users filled the days and often jammed the phone lines. It was as if everyone had been waiting for someone on whom to vent their frustrations. (Because of the living and working environment, these customers had little or no option to take their leisure needs elsewhere.) I had never encountered or heard of anything such as this before. To this day, I do not know why I did not get back on the plane and go home. The problems seemed insurmountable, and worse, there seemed to be no room to maneuver a solution.

Repeatedly, the administrators insisted that huge sums of money were earmarked for recreation improvements. But, it soon became clear that the previous recreation managers had all tried and failed, albeit halfheartedly, to get these funds released. Bureaucracy and red tape were so rampant that few individuals took responsibility for anything and, therefore, no checks were ever signed, no contracts filled out, and no works ever begun. Any earlier attempts had been lost in the system or were simply given up. In the meantime, executive committee members argued among themselves as to what to do.

Several months later, it was revealed that my job position had been available for some time. Nobody in Riyadh had bothered to apply. Why did I accept the position? Simply put, I needed a job and could not find a managerial position elsewhere. Having lived in Riyadh before, I was aware of the restrictions and customs, but I had never had to deal with them at the level encountered at the Hospital. It was only after the Gulf War that the crackdown on foreigners' liberal behavior began, and I was unaware of both that situation and the condition of the Hospital's recreation department despite a cursory investigation. The department's reputation, however, was well known. Although plans had originally been to stay for five to six years, it was clear this would not be the case. I decided to honor the two-year contract and do as much as possible before moving on. This would prove to be the most challenging (and frustrating) endeavor I have ever undertaken.

Reprinted at the end of this essay is an actual memo written two months after my arrival to the Hospital and Recreation Services. It is an example of the external problems we were up against. *While situations such as this did not happen regularly,* the *threat* of them occurring was very real. With numerous activities scheduled per day, which lasted well into the night, it was not uncommon to find myself at home at the end of the day casting a wary eye at the telephone waiting for "that telephone call." If there was to be any trouble, it was customary in Saudi Arabia for all the participants to be detained until the problem was sorted out. The head of Recreation Services would be held accountable. No hospital administrator would ever admit responsibility. Complaints, usually culture-based, could erupt with any of our programs or activities. Often the department pager was switched off to enable a good night's sleep. (People were known to page me at two o'clock in the morning with complaints.)

Our leisure business was not the only one that had to put up with arrogant expatriates and difficult cultural restrictions. The assistant head of Recreation Services at a nearby hospital was once taken to the religious enforcement headquarters and questioned for an entire afternoon. A file was presented, bulging with brochures and posters colorfully advertising the activities his department had provided over the years. He was told to explain each one, including the children's birthday parties. He was sternly warned that these activities contradicted their religious beliefs, lectured on religious practices, forced to sign a statement promising to comply with them, and then released. Problems regarding the conflicts between Western and Saudi culture arose on a daily basis, and while most were minor, they did grow wearisome. Recreation Services was made to deal with these situations more so than most other departments because we were the link between the Hospital's boundaries and outside realities. These outside forces caused great concern and even fear among all of us. This environment was the one to which our transformational change would have to take place.

MEMORANDUM

TO: Mr. Jonathan T. Scott
                 Recreation Coordinator, Club

THROUGH: Director, Club

FROM:

DATE: 20 Shawwal 1413   (April 12, 1993)

SUBJ: HERITAGE AND CULTURAL EXHIBITION
                 AT AL-JANADRIYAN

I was dismayed to see the above readvertised this year. I was one of the unfortunate women who made the mistake of joining this tour, and I had persuaded a few of my friends to accompany me. You may not be aware that this afternoon last year was a total fiasco.

When we arrived at Al-Janadriyah we were met with the sight of an expatriate male being separated from his spouse at the entrance gate and taken away in handcuffs. To gain entry to the exhibition, some of the Hospital women were required to open their abayas to let the Mutawa and "security" personnel ensure that "nothing was concealed." We were roughly jostled, our handbags were repeatedly searched (personally four times upon entry and three times on leaving). As I had a shoulder strap type of bag, it was ripped from my person and searched.

Whilst inside the exhibition, the harassment continued for some and four Hospital women were physically kicked, punched, and left with bruises as souvenirs of their day's outing. I understand that one of the injured women wrote about the incident to Dr. Jabbar and the American Embassy.

We were repeatedly shouted at to cover our heads and cover our faces. This was almost the most awful day I have experienced in Riyadh, and as far as I was concerned, certainly not typical of the Saudi heritage and culture that I have come to learn from Saudis I work with.

I think that by advertising this exhibition you are putting at risk unsuspecting women (like myself and many others last year). If the same force of Mutawa and "security" personnel will be in attendance, you are inviting Hospital women to a frightening experience along with possible personal injury.

cc: Counsel and Supervisor of Executive Management, Chief Executive
     Director
     Chairman, Department of _____

PART II:
THEORIES AND APPLICATIONS

Introduction

Take another look at the case study introduction. The situations mentioned are not that unique. National and local laws, regulations and customs; hostile customers, customers who are unaware of or ignore legal guidelines and restrictions; lack of available funds; an unmotivated workforce; unpopular programs and activities; the need to drastically increase revenues; accumulating problems; an uncaring or incompetent administration—do these situations sound familiar? Most leisure organizations will encounter one or more versions of these problems throughout their business lives. Inevitably, these types of problems will arise when there may appear to be no apparent solutions or when there is no room to maneuver. The question then is: "What can be done?"

Mention theories and applications to most seasoned business practitioners, and eyes immediately begin to roll at this academic intrusion into business realities. Is not reading and writing about work-related problems something only college professors have the time for? Professionals in leisure businesses want workable solutions that can be developed and implemented straightaway. Customers will not wait while the business sorts itself out. When jobs and market share are on the line, who has time for theories?

Well, as a die-hard practitioner myself, I used to think along those lines. After all, when Recreation Services eventually improved, it was done so without any theories—or so I thought. Leading a successful turnaround gave me the confidence to enroll in business school, but I always assumed I would not learn much of anything that experience had not taught. I wanted an MBA so that I would be considered more employable. In the age-old argument regarding which is more important, education or experience, I always took the experience side of the debate (and still do to some degree). However, there has been a change in my thinking.

Studying the works of others shined a light on many of the unpleasant situations that had occurred while working in the Hospital and in Saudi Arabia. It clarified things and helped me to better understand why certain applications work and why people behave as they do. Most important, I was instilled with confidence when I listened to how others faced similar, or worse, challenges and came out on top. Surprisingly, the same practices they used turned out to be a reflection of what Recreation Services did to improve itself—the same information and theories that business professionals have been writing and talking about for years.

Taking on any new task is a lot like groping in a darkened room for a light switch. The less information or experience you have with the layout of the room, the harder your search for illumination becomes. Learning about change management better prepares both the individual and the group for the difficulties that lie ahead when making improvements and understanding their implications. One of the most important success-inducing tools in any business is relevant, factual, and reliable information.

This section contains a relatively brief two-year case study of the Recreation Services transformational changes. It is divided into seven information-filled categories, accumulated from business academic leaders, that help present the case study, change, and basic business concepts in a logical fashion. These categories, administered and balanced correctly, are what many individuals believe to be that which makes successful organizations stay successful. Mind you, this information is not a prescription. It is relayed in the hopes that it can be *adapted* to your individual needs and those of your leisure business.

Building the Commitment to Change

(TRANSFORMATION BEGINS . . .)

Change is inevitable and is almost always resisted. In order for effective change to be implemented and take hold within an organizational structure, breadth and depth is required. Breadth means that the change takes place across the entire organization, every department and area must take part, from the executive office down to the stock room. Depth means that every individual within these areas—from top management to shop worker—becomes involved in, and is aware of, what is going on and why.

Initiating change is often a gut-wrenching experience. Corporate executives have been known to be reduced to tears, and managers to despair, when change is thrust upon them. Barriers and old habits within the organization are broken and rearranged. Often the very culture of an institution is reorganized. People will frequently try to resist any changes, whether consciously or subconsciously. This is usually because of the fear change creates. The following text is adapted from William Band's *Creating Value for Customers* (1991) and explains the source of these fears and the reactions one is likely to encounter in administering transformation.

Fear of loss of control	Change requires people to go from being certain of things to being uncertain and out of control.
Too much uncertainty	The future is not obvious, and it feels as if you are about to walk off a cliff every day. This leads to many employees wanting details, contingencies, and examinations. Watch out for "paralysis by analysis."

Too many surprises	People like novelty, but hate surprises. Early warnings are necessary to avoid unwanted shocks.
We love our habits	Habits are efficient, effective, and mindless. Change will be uncomfortable.
Need for familiarity	Everybody likes what is familiar. We feel comfortable going back to places we know.
New things mean more work	True, especially in the beginning, but this often subsides and tasks can become easier and more efficient (often the reason for change).
Concern for competence	People often question their ability to master new skills, particularly if training and ongoing support are not provided or are viewed with skepticism.
Lack of skills	New tasks require people to learn skills they do not have. These are sometimes perceived as being difficult to acquire.
Time to adjust	Saying "do it differently" is not enough. It takes time for new skills and a sense of comfort to develop. Rushing can lead to disruption, sabotage, resistance, and poor performance.

Transition can be greatly eased by using the following methods:

- Involve as many people as possible. Participation leads to ownership, enthusiasm, and motivation.
- Communicate clearly and often. Provide as much detail as possible.

- Divide changes into manageable, comprehensive steps. Make these steps as familiar as possible. Make them small and easy, and try your best to make sure they are successful.
- Allow for no surprises.
- Let commitment grow. Do not ask for a pledge of allegiance to new and untried ways.
- Make clear what will be expected of people during and after the change. Fully communicate standards and requirements.
- Provide all the *continuous* training needed.

Recreation Services at the Hospital was ripe for a change. Most of the staff welcomed any new ideas designed to make improvements, but its internal past history, and in particular the external environment, would make these changes difficult. The greatest fear was what the reaction would be by the wary administration. Rather than pause over any personal implications or delve into too much analysis, the plunge was made, and an attack on all fronts began . . .

Strategy

Strategy refers to a plan or course of action that leads to the allocation of a firm's scarce resources, over time, to reach identified goals (Pascale, 1991). In essence this means the plan for getting where the organization is, to where it wants to go. Because things were in such a poor state at Recreation Services, it was difficult to decide where to begin. My first reaction was to simply order and purchase materials and equipment to inject the programs and activities with a much needed boost. Within the first week however, it became clear that an assessment of the lack of safety measures needed immediate attention. From there, a rough format emerged more or less in the following order of desired goals:

ADDRESS SAFETY CONCERNS

Recreation Services had eleven swimming pools, none of which had any safety equipment. With only minor hesitation from the Club, funds were released on an emergency basis to buy the floats, hooks, ropes, signs, and locks for the pool areas. All recreation staff were required to participate in and pass an intensive two-day CPR course sponsored by the Red Cross. (The Red Cross operates with great secrecy, lest the religious fundamentalists see the "offensive" logo and the word "cross.") Training was paid for with petty cash funds, as the Club did not wish to meet this expense. In addition, arrangements were made for a Hospital paramedic to give a training session to all staff concerning what steps to take in an emergency situation. An immediate search began for a female lifeguard. (Male lifeguards are not allowed near pools during "ladies' times.") Emergency numbers were posted at all telephones, and work orders were put in to repair all broken phones. Broken and outdated equipment was disposed of or stored for disposal (due to red tape, it often took *one to two years* for items to be given clearance for disposal), and on several occasions, many old chemicals, discarded materials, and dangerous items were clandestinely stored in the trunk of my car and smuggled past Hospital security to various rubbish bins in the city. We simply could not have these things on the premises, and the stockrooms and facilities were literally heaving with this junk. All staff were continually reminded that someone had lost their life due to our unsafe practices and this could not continue.

Without question, the one policy that created the most aggravation to both myself and the staff was the enforcement of the badge policy. All Hospital employees and their dependents were issued ID badges to be worn at all times for security reasons, especially at recreation facilities. This policy had been ignored over the years, and when many of the employees who had wandered on and off recreation grounds with no IDs were told the policy was now being enforced, quite literally all hell broke loose. Pools and other facilities now being locked after hours simply added to the furor.

The amount of shouting, nasty memos, obscene phone calls, physical violence, and abuse from the Hospital workforce was astounding. Many times the staff were reduced to tears, as both they and I were subjected to the most horrific verbal abuse imaginable. Shockingly, some of the staff were even threatened with job loss and assault to their families all because the staff members politely asked for an ID badge to be presented before entry to facilities. (The drowning victim had not been a hospital employee or dependent.)

Despite an executive order demanding employees wear their badges, the hospital administration and, sadly, the Club rarely if ever gave any help with this matter except when physical violence erupted. We were told to just carry out the policy. Often enough these same administrators would phone our offices asking for us to overlook this policy so that their unauthorized friends and family could be admitted after we had previously denied them entry. Eventually, by the second year, the amount of protest died out when employees learned that we could not and would not compromise. Providing basic safety and security proved to be the greatest nightmare we would all have to face.

ESTABLISH WORK GUIDELINES

It was clear from the outset that it would not be possible to directly supervise the forty-seven recreation staff members at the sixteen different recreation sites (twelve recreation sites plus four service sites). Besides being physically impossible, time needed to be spent on several different problem areas, not just employee supervision. A policy was established whereby each employee was required to present *at least* three quality activities per day. Since activities only lasted about two hours, and ten-hour workdays were mandatory (according to our contracts), this allowed plenty of time for program development, organization, and implementation.

Recreation staff were given complete empowerment to develop their own programs. All staff members had the skills, education, and experience to run recreation programs. Now they were required to coordinate their own planning, work time, and program schedules. Activities had to: (1) be high quality, (2) attract at least six participants, and (3) be varied. At first, the six-person limitation was overlooked, as we often had fewer participants enrolled for our activities. Customers had been so used to things being canceled, we tried not to cancel anything during the first year. This significantly boosted confidence with the clientele.

Although the staff were at first quite timid with their newfound freedom, they eventually came through and performed beyond all expectations. This required months and months of encouragement, with some employees making faster gains than others. Restrictions were also set as to when I could be contacted on the personal pager I was required to wear twenty-four hours a day, seven days a week. It was made clear that this was for emergency purposes only, not to have me solve all minor work-related problems.

Communication was stressed repeatedly both individually and at every staff meeting so that everyone knew what was going on and could function as a team. Communication was considered a vital part of everyday work. This included telephone etiquette toward customers. Everyone was aware of the restrictions the Saudi environment demanded so training was established to encourage individual and team confidence within these perimeters. Much of this became self-training, and together with the simple and clear expectations of the work guidelines, this proved to be one of the most fulfilling of the goals obtained. It is always a pleasure to watch people grow and create professionally. *Undoubtedly, it also led to many future improvement approvals being procured.*

CLEAN ALL FACILITIES

The cleaning of the sixteen locations was done by four men, three of whom could not speak English. Along with the cleaning of these sites for safety reasons, it was realized that cleanliness would attract more customers and would prepare these areas for any anticipated renovations. Major cleanups were ordered at all sites, and when it became apparent that I was visiting each location three or four times per week (management by walking around), the cleaning crews began to put more effort into their work. Our sole English-speaking maintenance man (who, it was discovered, held a degree in Civil Engineering), took on the additional responsibility of supervising and scheduling these men. Maintenance problems could then be dealt with directly when they were discovered by the cleaners. Things went fairly smoothly, though obviously, four men were never quite able to keep up with the maintenance demand. Pleas for more cleaners (easily affordable at U.S. $100 per month!) went ignored. We made do with what we had.

ORDER NEEDED EQUIPMENT

Because no materials had been purchased in years, the number of programs and activities we could offer was severely limited. It took months of persuasion to obtain the approval for the purchase of a myriad of recreation items, and the first order was a big one, over $7,000 worth. Employees did not have to be reminded to care for this equipment. The items were treated like fine jewelry and put in *their* trust and care. A system was set up to keep track of the inventory, which involved the input and the responsibility of the workforce, and the ordering of new supplies occurred about every four months. "Wish lists" from the staff were easy to sort out. No one was extravagant, and the rise in diversity and program numbers (and participants) ensured that equipment orders would be approved in the future.

RENOVATE AND CONSTRUCT FACILITIES

All facilities were in need of renovation (several needed it desperately), and in some cases, they greatly needed expansion as well. This is where most of my energy and attention was focused. The cost of these improvements would be in the hundreds of thousands of dollars. Outside construction contractors specializing in recreation facilities would have to be called in; inspections, budgets, and estimates considered; proposals needed to be made; and bids entered. This had never been successful in the past. The red tape and bureaucracy had proven to be too much. This time, however, an inordinate amount of persistence and team effort paid off. Most areas were eventually improved, and a detailed description of these undertakings are discussed in the "Skills" section.

DEVELOP NEW PROGRAMS AND ACTIVITIES

Once the new equipment had arrived and the staff became more settled with the additional amount of control they had with their positions and responsibilities, further emphasis was placed on expanding and improving our programs and activities. "The objective of total quality is to create an organization where everyone is working to make that organization the best in its field. To do this requires empowering the people and giving them the opportunity to tackle the problems they recognize and have the skills to solve" (Hutchins, 1992). Most of the staff had been in the employ of Recreation Services for years and understood the needs and desires of the people they served. With new confidence, partly inspired by being listened to, they were strongly encouraged to pursue their own ideas and innovations, as well as those from customers, to offer as part of our program. Providing ownership of work is the safe way to obtain job security, creativity, and flexibility (Stewart, 1994), and this certainly held true with the staff. The sheer number and variety of our activities, programs, and trips obtained unprecedented highs.

STRATEGY IS A . . .

1. *Plan*—a direction or course of action into the future.
2. *Pattern*—the consistency of behaviors.
3. *Position*—where your business, product, or service is in relation to others.
4. *Perspective*—how the organization perceives itself and its vision.

Planning the pathways of safety, work guidelines, facility clean-ups, equipment purchases, facility improvements/construction, and program development required an understanding of both the internal and external workings of the organization's frameworks. This is sometimes represented graphically by what is called a SWOT analysis (Strengths, Weaknesses, Opportunities, Threats). Strengths and weaknesses are concerned primarily with internal factors, while opportunities and threats relate to external influences. Putting these into perspective: (1) allows for the coordination of strategy; (2) ensures the future is taken into account; (3) enables rationalization to be involved ("strategic thinking rarely occurs spontaneously") (Porter, 1987); and (4) allows for better control of the business. In other words, these portray the very definition of effective planning. (Note that some entries are interchangeable.)

SWOT Analysis can be quite detailed, but the previous example adequately displays the challenges and means that lay ahead for the Recreation Services Department within the Hospital's structure. Some-

STRENGTHS	WEAKNESSES
(Internal)	
Skilled staff	Highly bureaucratic structure
Much money allocated for improvements	Inadequate/poorly maintained facilities
	Low morale
Willingness to take some risks	Very poor perception of Recreation Services
Administration interested in leisure	
Crisis situation (change needed)	Lack of leadership/direction
Separate budget and accounts	An apathetic administration
	Distrust of recreation management

OPPORTUNITIES	THREATS
(External)	
Inconsistent enforcement of laws/customs	Hospital administrative "meddling"
Possible links to outside leisure businesses	Enforcement of strict religious practices
	Inconsistent enforcement of laws/customs
Separate budget and accounts	Unfriendly clientele
Desire and room for improvement	Very poor perception of Recreation Services
	Recreation Services viewed as separate from the Hospital

times formulating strategies can be difficult because of numerous unseen factors and the ever changing environment that affect the organization. Too much planning can produce restrictions that snuff out any creative sparks. Still, some form of vision and direction must be realized. As no master plan was used for the completion of the department's goals (this section is written with much hindsight), the initial "how-to" strategy was to strive toward informality and become more adaptable—in other words, break down as many walls and barriers as possible. As the old saying goes, "If faced with uncertainty—remain flexible." Interestingly, as the remaining categories ("Seven S's") are explored, the relation of strategy to other pertinent organizational elements becomes more clear.

Structure

Structure refers to the way a firm is organized. In short, how the chain of command "boxes" are arranged. [These are] the salient features of the organizational chart and how the separate entities are tied together. (Pascale, 1991)

The structural limitations the Club was forced to endure within the Hospital's framework provided some of the more difficult problems Recreation Services encountered. The bureaucratic pathways involved in getting approvals, answers, or information could take weeks, months, or even years. Writing memos was the favored method of communication. Few people seemed to want to use the phone or worse, try talking face to face. At times we would receive memos that wound their way around the administrative offices acquiring initials and signatures, only to find that what was being written about had already happened. Everyone had a separate opinion as to the proper completion of forms and processes. Worse still were the departments that operated as separate islands, refusing to cooperate with other individuals or departments because their employees did not like them.

When the Club was formed, many Hospital department heads took it upon themselves to sever any formal links with the new organization. The fact that the Club had its own budget only added to their beliefs that Club workers were separate and did not merit their attention. This occurred despite the Club remaining a vital part of the Hospital with all the paperwork, forms, approvals, purchases, and activities that still required the Hospital's regular, bureaucratic processes. It was common for individuals holding a management or supervisory position in a department to complain or make suggestions on certain matters that necessitated this very same department's help, coordination, or approval. When this was then asked for, the response was inevitably, "Sorry, can't help you. You're the

Club." This back-and-forth "we are a part of the Hospital, we are not a part of the Hospital" was never resolved and, despite many attempts, would not be discussed by the chairman of the executive committee board. The club director phrased it well when he told the Hospital's chief executive director, "We would like to be considered a part of the Hospital family rather than its stepchild." (Separation would later be used to our benefit. See "Skills—Exercise Gym.")

Our complaints fell on deaf ears, and many problems had to be solved by formulating alliances and friendships with the individuals responsible for the services we needed. This proved to be very effective. With the staff's help, the recreational interests of key people were discovered, and these interests were then played upon in order to solicit help on planned projects or day-to-day functions. For example, it was relatively easy to gather a formidable force of tennis-playing top surgeons and administrators to help push the tennis court improvement proposals through. Those in charge of maintenance loved to play squash and provided the required inspections and memos to complete work there. Individuals in high-ranking positions at many residential compounds were enlisted for improvements to the facilities located at these sites. Several willingly (and gleefully) wrote "complaints" addressed to the Club's chairman and board after members were privately told that was where the holdup was. (There is nothing like numerous well-placed complaints to initiate action.) Handing out free golf passes to key individuals did not hurt either. In fact, going through other channels sometimes proved to be more effective and efficient.

Within the Recreation Services itself, the structure changed significantly. In the past, all problems, questions, and concerns were relayed directly to the department head. "Quality teams are structured [to] accept ownership for solutions" (Barry, 1991), so by delegating responsibilities directly to those providing our activities, many problems were solved "on site." As the staff learned to solve their own problems, answer questions, and in effect, handle responsibility, the organization became "flatter" and contributed to the improvement of customer services. This included the emphasis on interdepartmental communication. The business terminology of such practices is often referred to as decentralization.

When an organization or business becomes flatter, what is meant is that there are fewer people, departments, processes, and bureaucracy between the customer and the employees within the organization who make decisions. In essence, customers can be served faster and more efficiently because the person(s) responsible for information and making decisions deals with them directly. If the customers are considered to be everyone within the business as well as those with outside contacts, then the hierarchy and barriers of company structure must be torn down to facilitate the flow of information required for everyone to do their jobs well. The result is that those traditionally at the top move closer to the customer, and those who in the past considered themselves as "just working here" learn to think and respond.

Because we could not obtain formal directives for our role in the Hospital's structure, we accomplished this by becoming closer to those we served. We unashamedly let the customers become involved and occasionally told them that we needed their help from time to time. Through this "community" involvement, we ultimately achieved our aims. In a unique way, we became part of the Hospital's structure by reaching up through the bottom of its organizational structure rather than coming down from the top. Different teams could take on a number of problems at once, and our humility generated much help. People love to give their advice and when they become involved, well, "many hands make light work." Flattened organizational structures help acquire improvements and success.

Systems

Systems pertain to procedures and rationalized processes; in other words, how information used to keep track of what is going on moves within the organization (Pascale, 1991). This includes written materials, information displays, and meetings.

Systems within Recreation Services improved markedly during the first year. Internally, the lines of communication were made open and accessible. For example, memo writing was kept to a minimum, and person-to-person communication was encouraged. Externally, the information posted to our clientele through the publishing of a monthly activity bulletin became more informative and professional-looking, and we began acting on our customers' advice and suggestions. This increased the staff's knowledge, and the improvement in incoming communications became improvements that extended back out to our customers.

Here the term "customer" is used in its broadest sense. Oakland (1993) sees customers as being all the individuals within the organizational framework (colleagues, secretaries, contractors, etc.), as well as those whose business is being sought. Taken into perspective, this means that *everyone* we come into contact with is, in effect, a customer. *Knowing what the customers' requirements are greatly contributes to improved quality.* However, this knowledge cannot be acquired without effective communication, or in other words, asking just what it is the customer wants. For us, an increase in training and work-related knowledge produced an improved information system that quickly brought information from within the business to outside customers and in turn brought external information to the appropriate individuals within the organization.

Although the delegation and empowerment of work-related functions were being handed over to the staff, the reasons for doing so were not initially to improve the system with our clientele. This had been done in order to free up enough time to pursue construction contracts and fight for project funding. The unexpected side effect was that decisions and answers to questions could now be given on site by the recreation employees themselves. Customers did not have to wait for the staff to get back to them with an answer after seeking management's response. This proved to be particularly beneficial in our main office, where many inquiries were directed.

In the past, office staff routinely could not respond to questions or give out required information. Many just did not know what was going on in the department. Frustrations from customers mounted as staff telephone numbers were given out, and the search for someone with the correct information (often simple and basic information) began. If staff members were indeed responsible for certain programs, no one knew where they were, when they would be back, when their activities would be, or where they were located.

To solve the problem, an enormous white board was mounted on one of the main office's walls. Every staff member's name was listed on this board, as well as a space next to it with column headings labeled: location, time out, and time in. The remaining half of the board listed the day's activities, trips, and programs in sequential order with the venues, employees off duty, those on holiday (and when they were returning), as well as a space for any pertinent daily information. The department secretary was trained to fill this board in *every* morning before anything else was done. It took weeks to get the staff to sign in and out, but once accomplished, the amount of "I don't knows" relayed to our clientele was greatly reduced.

Information posted on the notice boards had to be professional looking and displayed attractively. Staff were encouraged to periodically check if this was the case rather than just walking past. All notices were removed after two weeks of display. No signs were to be posted on walls or doors. Filing cabinets and storage areas were searched for antiquated forms and memos that were then thrown out. (At one time, a security guard found a three-year-old memo instructing a facility to be closed down because of the Gulf War. He then acted upon it and shut a much used facility down for half the day!) Filing systems were upgraded and no one person was allowed to control information sheets, which had been the case in the past. Employees were asked to use their good judgment in making decisions (instead of waiting to ask) and then to tell everyone about it as soon as possible so we would all know what was going on.

Monthly meetings were held on a more consistent basis, and the tone of these radically changed. In the past, prior to my arrival, staff meetings were used primarily to scold or berate. Now they were used to discuss the status of ongoing projects, projected trouble spots, Club concerns, and other vital pieces of information so that we would be better prepared to work. Questions and concerns were encouraged and addressed, and brainstorming sessions became more prevalent.

As time went on, employees became more comfortable with the new format and began to use these meetings very effectively. Numerous suggestions and conflicts could then be addressed openly and constructively, and everyone's input could then be used and examined.

As we became better able to respond to customer inquiries, the primary source of relaying information, the "Recreation Bulletin," began to improve. Earlier, this monthly bulletin had caused many headaches. It took about two weeks to collect the employee's activity suggestions, sort through them, type them up, illustrate them, do a layout, make corrections, and submit the product to the print shop, which then took another week to print the bulletin. With none of the staff being native English speakers, and most being computer illiterate, the resulting product looked amateurish at best. We were fortunate to find a Western secretary who was more interested in productivity than in money.

Saudi culture leaves little for unemployed Western wives to do, and being cooped up all day while her husband was at work was taking its toll. Catherine, from Limerick, Ireland, took on the responsibility of producing the Recreation Bulletin, as well as the usual office tasks. Catherine was given free reign to initiate any improvements, and within several months, reduced the Recreation Bulletin's preparation time from two weeks to four or five days (allowing her extra time to develop and greatly enhance an international trips program!). "The first task of any advertising is to make the audience appreciate that the product or service exists and to explain exactly what it is" (Mercer, 1992), and this is what the Recreation Bulletin could finally do. Its smarter appearance, professional look, and reduction in grammatical and informational errors demonstrated to every one of our customers that things were changing. "I had no idea you offered so much until I saw the new Recreation Bulletin," said one customer.

However, the region we were in brought about interesting problems created by the Recreation Bulletin's new popularity. For some fundamentalists, the practice of not succumbing to graven images is taken to the extreme. The result is that any image is perceived as sacrilegious. Oil paintings, illustrations, art, and even cartoons and photographs can fall into this category. The monthly Recreation Bulletin relied heavily on small illustrations to draw attention to, and market, our recreation programs. Quite often some fundamentalist would find a drawing that he considered "offensive." The Recreation Bulletin would then have to be changed.

The problem was solved by substituting the "offensive" picture for one chosen by a conservative Saudi. Apparently any "graven image" beliefs could be superceded by having us relinquish picture-choosing authority!* Most important, the completed Recreation Bulletin could then be distributed with fewer problems.

The increased circulation of the Recreation Bulletin attracted more customers, reminded existing users of our services, reassured previous purchasers, countered the market decline, informed customers, announced benefits, increased revenues, launched new services, and proclaimed a myriad of other benefits in a new, user-friendly manner—all the important, effective, and desired objectives of proper marketing (Davis, 1988). (Sadly, Catherine left after one year, in part because of an American woman's relentless campaign of insults designed to discredit her for writing in British English terminology and spelling, rather than American English. All of the staff were behind her, but Catherine considered it

---

*Some of these "religious beliefs" could never be figured out. We had to remove a large oil painting painted by a Muslim staff member, depicting a pride of lions lying beneath a tree in the African Serengeti, from the exercise gymnasium's wall. However, photographs and posters of scantily clad bodybuilders never generated a single complaint. (This was in a country where men had to wear swimsuits that covered the thighs and upper arms, and could not swim in the company of women, who had to be completely covered.) Inconsistencies such as these often led to frustration from the expatriate workforce.

demeaning and simply decided it was just as easy to leave. I tried my best to rectify the situation to no avail. We received no help from the administration as well.)

Even new technology played a role in the organization's changes. Although the Hospital at first refused us permission to update an old, insufficient computer, perseverance paid off, and a new IBM desktop unit was eventually purchased. This proved to be a key moment in the Recreation Bulletin's upgrading, and most of the staff showed a keen interest in learning the desktop's operation. This interest was enthusiastically encouraged. Only one office employee refused to learn how to operate the new computer. It was then made mandatory for her to enroll in a Hospital-sponsored computer class, and once the fear of this new machine subsided, she began to experience benefits the new unit offered. The creativity shown in the employee's written materials improved dramatically. Information and communication, and their efficient use, reaped enormous benefits for our systems framework and began permeating throughout the entire organization. Of the numerous results that unfolded because of the advantages this provided, everyone's job was made that much easier as well.

Staff

Staff consists not in the line/staff sense, but to demographic characterizations of the kind of people who collectively comprise the organization. (Pascale, 1991)

The forty-seven individuals who comprised Recreation Services represented twelve different countries. Each had his or her own culture, religion, language or dialect, style of dress, accent, and particular way of doing things. "Managers need to be aware of how cultural differences can influence the attitudes and motivations of staff and their pace of work" (Mullins, 1992).

Having worked or lived among people with differing backgrounds before, I was aware of the attention to interpersonal relationships this scenario demands. Working within an international environment is truly rewarding and is anything but ordinary. Far from being troublesome, these differences created a vitality and uniqueness unmatched in most recreation and leisure businesses. The diversity of the staff only ensured creative solutions to problems, concerns, and day-to-day activities. Language was not a problem, as English is the common work language spoken in Saudi Arabia, and all staff members were fluent enough for the responsibilities each individual's job required. In addition, all employees had the knowledge and skills needed to perform their work functions; all positions are recruited and demand competent applicants. In fact, many were placed in positions that one might consider beneath their full potential. During my tenure, several were given promotions, and just about everyone was given a pay raise. This included an exceptionally competent man who, over two years, eventually rose to become a department assistant, having originally been hired years earlier as a pool cleaner. Another man, it was discovered, had a Bachelors Degree in Gymnastics and Physical Education. It did not take much convincing to have him develop programs centered around these activities.

Being blessed with a talented workforce was a major reason for the department's continuing success. For years these employees had worked under an exceptionally oppressive management whose apathy and complacency only added to the organization's misery. When they were finally given the chance to excel, this same staff blossomed into a productive unit. It seemed as if each one had something positive to prove. This is not to say the department did not suffer through the pains that change creates. We most certainly did. But, the bottom line is that we were continuously improving and were making conscientious decisions to do so as individuals and a team. "Teams sometimes have a higher commitment and set higher standards than managers would" (Band, 1991).

One day I was very anxious for a document to be written, when the computer deleted a large section of it. Romet Rinato, who had been working with the new computer, was used to its "teething pains" and was convinced this section was still stored somewhere in the computer's memory. It was vital to retrieve this information and send it off quickly, so imagine my surprise when Romet was discovered calmly smoking a cigarette on the pool veranda twenty minutes later, with the document still not finished. With anger rising, I bit my lip and returned to the office to become immersed in a contingency plan.

Thirty minutes later, Romet appeared in the doorway with the completed document. He had found the deleted section after walking away from the computer terminal in order to "clear (his) head and find time to think." Over the months, despite all we had gone through, or rather because of it, the staff had learned to use their time wisely. It was apparent by looking at the improvements in work quality that more time was being used to prepare their programs and that the staff were working smarter, not just harder. At the end of the day, it was common to see them still enjoying work despite their shift having ended. Given the chance, these people had taught themselves (and me) that becoming a part of an organization meant that they would become more interested and invest more effort. Earlier it would have been impossible to find the employees after hours—sometimes even during work hours.

Early on there was an incident that brought home to all employees the need to rethink their role in the transformational processes that had just begun. Frank was a respected tennis instructor, a successful children's swim team coach (he led the team to several national championships), and was perhaps our most amiable and popular staff member. One Friday, Frank was nowhere to be found. Sometime later, an angry phone call was received from the Club director. "Why was Frank teaching private tennis lessons on company time?" he demanded, and "Why can't you keep track of your own staff?" As it was unclear what was going on, I drove to a distant recreation site and waited for Frank. During this time, a young boy approached with a tennis racquet. Careful questioning uncovered Frank's private operation: charging customers five times the Club fee for lessons and pocketing the difference. When Frank finally arrived, he was calmly told to report to my office first thing Monday morning. In the meantime, I searched through the office files and found numerous reprimands and disciplinary reports. Frank had been caught and warned about this same offense for many years. Obviously this could not continue, and it was apparent that these reprimands had no effect. On Monday morning, he was fired.

Surprisingly, although the termination of employees was within the recreation head's authority, it took some convincing to get the Club administration's full support. This was accomplished by explaining that years of threats and warnings with no action were meaningless. Unfortunately, a mistake was made by persuading the administration to let Frank complete the month, at which time he could cash in on his accumulated contract severance benefits (a sizable amount).

Frank repaid me by spreading numerous malicious stories and accusations, painting himself as a hapless victim. The already overwhelming complaints we received only increased as Frank's customers and friends rushed to his defense. Quite a few people canceled their Club memberships in protest. Several times, I was harassed in public or over the telephone at my home; nobody wanted to hear the real reasons for Frank's termination. At some point, Frank began casting aspersions upon the Saudi administrators. Malicious gossip about me was one thing, but against the Saudis was another. He was immediately called to the executive offices. Fortunately, Frank had caught wind of the chairman's anger, and he was able to flee the country shortly before the police and customs officials were notified. He was on a plane to the United States as the search for him began.

Over the following months, numerous telephone calls were received from Frank's family overseas, begging for my intervention to try to release his accrued benefit pay and salary. Supposedly, his children were forced to leave school, he was going to lose his home, his family might starve, etc. By this time, the situation was thankfully out of my hands. Frank had sealed his fate by compounding his offenses after being offered an exceptionally generous severance package.

As the rest of the staff witnessed these theatrical incidents, it began to sink into the heads of the more stubborn ones that the changes taking place within the department were very real and did not just pertain to the physical improvements. Ignoring change could prove to be painful. Discipline, especially self-discipline, was needed if each individual wanted to survive the change process. From that moment on, everyone realized it was far easier to meet the new work requirements than to spend time and energy covering up questionable practices.

Despite some setbacks, particularly in the case of Frank's story, the majority of employees remained eager to improve the department and their role within it. The staff learned that sincere effort pays off; they were rewarded with fewer complaints, reduced stress and tension, hours or even days off with pay, and growing program recognition. Trained in the new organizational framework and armed with talent, skills, and the desire to use them to the best of their abilities, the employees could now be set free to be creative and show what they could do. It is often said that people are any organization's most important asset. Far from the lip service this statement unfortunately almost always receives, Recreation Services tried to use this concept to its fullest.

Style

Style refers to the patterns of behavior of the management. It also encompasses organizational traits and culture. (Pascale, 1991)

Nothing in the world can take the place of persistence. Talent will not; nothing is more common than the unsuccessful man with talent. Genius will not; unrealized genius is almost a cliché. Education will not; the world is full of educated derelicts. Persistence and determination alone are omnipotent. (Calvin Coolidge)

It had been less than two months since my arrival at the Hospital, and I was preparing for the Club's executive committee board meeting. I arrived early, trying to get away from the day's verbal abuses. My head was still reeling with them when Darla Cress, the board's nursing representative, entered the room. "I hear you're doing quite a bit over in Recreation," she said. I did not have a clue as to what she was talking about. Certainly nothing had been accomplished over the past few weeks, with the possible exception that I was now known as the Club's bull's-eye.

"Don't sell yourself short," Darla said. "Your consistency in standing up for your staff is already making the gossip rounds, and for the first time ever, they finally feel like someone is championing their cause." Darla proved to be right, and it only took a few moments to imagine what these people had suffered through previously. Often this was enough to bring me out of the depression that the seemingly overwhelming problems we faced frequently brought. Looking back, few other work-related problems carried the idea that we were a team and were all in this together.

"Leadership is a foul weather job. You cannot prevent a major catastrophe, but you can build an organization that is battle ready, that has high morale, that has been through crises, and has learned how to behave, trust itself, and trust one another" (Drucker, 1992). Nothing unites like a common enemy, and our enemy was the apathy, complacency, and lack of self-confidence that had established itself over time. If there was one trait that persevered over these and almost all other conflicts and problems, it was persistence—persistence and its consistent use in demanding that the staff be treated with civility, in pursuing approvals for construction and improvement projects, with needed purchases, with the enforcement of policies and new staff-inspired ideas, and with the belief that we could do better. This had more to do with our transformation than any other factor.

In the past, numerous plans and proposals had been entered into the Hospital's system with little more than a wing and a prayer. It was hoped that "the system" would carry out all the necessary approvals, signatures, and coordination required. If not, it was always convenient to blame any proposal's failure on "the system." It was instilled into the staff that one must follow a proposal as it winds its way through the organization AND NOT TO STOP until that proposal has been followed through completely. Our Sudanese martial arts instructor nicknamed me the "pounding man" (a rough translation of the term he used) because I would keep pounding away at something until it was finished.

One trait that gained attention was the establishment of an ethical stance. It was common for gifts, vouchers, freebies, and other offers to be surreptitiously asked for by those who previously held my position in exchange for providing exhibitions. This was *in addition* to a standard exhibition fee. Some of these "presents" were quite substantial; the Club director for example was given a new twenty-seven-inch color television set in exchange for allowing Panasonic to give an exhibition. Giving small thank-you gifts or doing small favors for others within the Hospital's structure in order to gain assistance was one thing, but outright bribery was wrong.

Abolishing this practice did not stop these "gifts" from coming in, but they were reduced considerably when outside vendors slowly realized they were not necessary in order to do business with us. Our relationship with these outside interests improved dramatically. We used to have to chase after these vendors. Now exhibitions provided by vendors and outside businesses rose to such an extent that there was a *three-month* waiting period of advanced bookings. Any gifts presented to me were considered to be donations to the department and were used as prizes for our contests and tournaments. Any other small personal gifts were considered the property of the staff member who received them. This probably marked the first time any employee had seen a recreation manager act without greed or selfishness.

Another style that produced staff respect was the informal manner with which the department was now being operated and the fact that employees' ideas were encouraged and implemented. My office door was always open, and an active interest was taken in the work the staff was doing. Full credit was given to those who had new innovations and ideas. Recreation is by its very nature open, informal, and rewarding, and that is the type of organizational structure for which we strived. Employees learned to do their own thing, accept ownership of their work, and at the same time, work together as one unit. I tried as much as possible to not let any stress or undue force come down on them from my office or indeed other offices. At the same time, it was always made clear that we could not lose sight of our goal of constant improvement.

One day during a regularly scheduled monthly staff meeting, everyone was surprised by the presence of a large cake and a table full of biscuits, sweets, and soft drinks. It was a personal thank-you for the staff's hard work. In addition, each staff member received a specially designed certificate, which had been secretly arranged with the print shop, declaring that the person mentioned had contributed substantially to the vast improvement of Recreation Services. While handing them out, a few complimentary words were given concerning each individual's achievements.

Successful business leaders recognize that managing fairly and consistently, through the use of carefully planned goals and a purposeful mission, helps substantially to establish a strong base from which prosperous transformation can take place. Although a mission statement was mistakenly never conceived for Recreation Services, a constant communication of our specific goals and the persistence in trying to achieve them gave direction and purpose to our organization (as did a reward system for a job well done).

There are many ways in which style involves itself within an organization's culture. Charles Handy (1993) describes six "style" methods of influence used in leadership roles in order to exert authority.

1. *Force.* This is the crudest method. It derives from physical power and ranges from threats to bullying.
2. *Rules and Procedures.* A person in power can influence a subordinate to do something by developing and enforcing these. Society uses them in the form of laws, and we are all subject to them at one time or another from childhood to old age.
3. *Exchange.* Bargaining, negotiating, and even cajoling or bribery fall under this category. Promotions, pay raises, friendship and favor, group inclusion and approval, and status are more subtle examples.
4. *Persuasion.* This is usually the first method of choice. In practice, however, it is usually contaminated by one of the other methods. Subordinates should be fully aware of their role in any work-related scenario and require relevant information, as to how they will benefit in order for persuasion to be used.
5. *Ecology.* All organizations are influenced by their environment. Using this environment effectively can create enormous influences. The use of a crisis to achieve a goal is an extreme example. If creativity is required from the workforce, then an environment that encourages this must be established. Ecology influences behaviors and allows other methods of influence to work.
6. *Magnetism.* This relates to the application of personal power. Wanting to work and perform for someone because he or she is charismatic is not easily measured, but it exists nonetheless. This can sometimes be witnessed in its abuse stages coming from faith healers, salesmen, etc.

The methods of influence used at Recreation Services prior to 1993 primarily rested with the use of force, rules, and procedures. This style is not conducive to a leisure-based organization or its atmosphere. Progress came about by eliminating the use of force and rules as much as possible and embracing the exchange, persuasion, and ecology methods of influence to create work incentives. Only after some major victories in the form of increased productivity, reduced complaints, and facility enhancements did magnetism come into play. This is magnetism in the departmental sense, as we all began to look like winners. This movement from the first of the six influence methods toward the center and end of the list is the style or pattern of behavior of management that became another key component in achieving desired results.

To be sure, there were moments when tempers were lost and personal motivation was lacking, but in the end, the consistency of these principles won the staff over. A letter I received from a friend after I had left the Hospital stated that the staff were using me as a measuring stick to gauge the new manager and that the staff continuously asked about my whereabouts. It can be difficult to be impartial when relaying how staff think of you, but I was always under the impression that I had sometimes been a bit hard on everyone. However, expecting more from individuals and convincing them that they are capable of more is not being "hard." Fairness, self-respect, understanding, and a commitment to doing better are values we all learned to care about throughout Recreation Services. Apparently that is the impression that rubbed off on the staff, as well as the style that is remembered.

Shared Values

... pertains to the overarching purposes to which an organization and its members dedicate themselves. These are never bottom line secular goals such as growing 10 percent a year or obtaining a 20 percent return on investment. Shared values tend to move men's hearts and knit individual and organization purposes together. (Pascale, 1991)

In many ways, shared values were an extension and addition to the goals and strategies used to improve Recreation Services. Simply put, they were to provide a better service and develop our work areas into something of which all of us would be proud. As simple as they sound, the sharing of values had never before been accomplished in the past, mainly because an organizational change was necessary for their implementation. As in the case of most value perceptions, what was at first thought to be of value was only the tip of the iceberg.

Terrence Deal and Allen Kennedy (1988) maintain that values are the bedrock of any corporate culture. Values provide a sense of common direction for all employees. If they are strong, they command everyone's attention. However, values are not concrete, and often they are not written down. Since organizational values can powerfully influence what people actually do, it was clear that Recreation Services could not suffer from value uncertainty. Value was placed on individual achievement and program and facility improvements. This required a change of cultures.

In 1972, Roger Harrison developed four separate organization cultures:

1. *The Power Culture.* Based on key individuals who generate almost complete control from their center. There are few rules and procedures and little bureaucracy. Power cultures can

move quickly and react well. However, if the key individuals are removed the cultures are extremely vulnerable.

2. *The Role Culture.* Often stereotyped as bureaucracy although not in its negative connotations. (Bureaucracy was originally established to eschew favoritism.) Coordination is maintained by a narrow band of senior management personnel. Performance over and above the role is not needed. Personal power is frowned upon, as rules and procedures are the major methods of influence. Written standards need only be met and the structure is rigid and formal.

3. *The Task Culture.* Project oriented. Emphasis is on getting the job done. Attention is given to skills; put the right people in the right position and let them get on with it. Results oriented, this culture is very adaptable. Task cultures thrive where creativity, competitiveness, short product life, and speed are required.

4. *The Person Culture.* The individual is the center point. These organizations exist only because those within them are "doing their own thing." Lawyers, physicians, and university professors are good examples of those working within a person culture.

By this time, it should be apparent that a shift from a role culture to a task culture was taking place within Recreation Services. Flexibility is an important aspect of a task culture. Flexibility was the inner environment we needed, especially in Saudi Arabia. Almost anything could happen at any time that would obstruct the goals of leisure. We needed adaptability without enormous expertise, influence rather than power. A task culture was perfectly suited and was used to the most benefit. Management could then concentrate on resource allocation, the placement of people, and their motivation.

Refusing to accept complacency, being overwhelmingly persistent toward our goals, and taking advantage of any opportunities, no matter how eye raising, initiated substantial change. Recreation Services' transformation broke through the barriers that had led to previous restrictions. Limitations began to be tested as hearts and minds set out to explore new possibilities. With little room to maneuver, one must always be as creative or as clever as possible, even to the point of overt risk taking. Some toes were stepped on at certain times, but the development of professional alliances within the Hospital's organization helped to smooth over any bruised egos, enabling favorable results. By not going it alone, our department accomplished the projects that every earlier manager or management team had failed to complete or even begin. Taking well-prepared risks paid off handsomely.

At an individual level, the staff members each had the skills to establish a diverse recreation service. At an organizational level, we learned to function within a framework as a team. Respect and dignity began to permeate the organization. Sometimes I feel that the department having been in such a mess contributed to the drive for all of us to improve. There are examples in business case studies of administrators who actually create a crisis in order to develop the conflicts needed to wake everyone up and get people and ideas moving. We most certainly had our own crises to confront, and by continuously convincing everybody that we had to face our own problems and could do better, the use of this concept became instrumental.

Richard Pascale (1991), through research and a series of interviews, wondered just what it took for true transformation to take hold and remain. He believes that the harnessing of tension and contention is the key and concludes that all successful change initiatives hold three things in common:

1. Transformation requires an attack on many different fronts.
2. Different situations require different leadership strategies.
3. Serendipity almost always applies. There is no "Master Plan."

Constructive conflict is seen as the means to maintaining successful change. Otherwise, the organization could grow complacent. Constructive conflict deals functionally with problems and confrontations and bravely faces the often valid concerns that arise from them. When this was finally realized, it is astonishing to see that the methods of success in revitalizing Recreation Services matched the same principles that brought about the successful transformation of corporate giants. Our haphazard way of trying different strategies, using different approaches suited to differing problems, attacking problems at various levels all at once, forming teams and alliances, and curiously, not really planning any of it proved to be highly effective. There was also plenty of conflict about to keep the creative ideas and solutions flowing. Appropriately, using the compilation of the diverse skills available in conjunction with Pascale's transformation requirements was undeniably that which set us apart from any "competition." Handy's (1993) "best fit" approach graphically shows different aspects of the "Seven S's" (here displayed using four categories) and how they can fit together as a whole. Handy's scale is quite adequate; his contention is that there are four sets of factors an organization must take into consideration. These are:

1. *Leader*—his or her preferred style of operating and any personal characteristics.
2. *Subordinates*—their preferred style of leadership in light of the circumstances.
3. *Task*—the job, its objectives, and its technology.
4. *Environment*—the organizational setting of the leader, the group, and the importance of the task.

"The 'best fit' theory maintains that there is no such thing as the right style of leadership, but that leadership will be most effective when the requirements of the leader, the subordinates, and the task fit together" (ibid). This can be demonstrated on a scale running from tight to flexible:

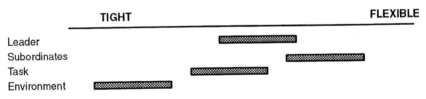

Handy uses his own version of the Seven S's by further simplifying the structure of an organization and dividing it into four categories: Leader (manager), Subordinates (nonmanagement employees), Task (work requirements), and Environment (competitive, physical, cultural, and/or legal surroundings). He then uses a scale showing the extremes by which each of the four categories can operate—either rigidly or "tight" with no room for alteration, adaptation, or questions (bureaucracy or military-type command would be an example), or with great flexibility (anything or everything is accepted).

Different change situations demand that the four categories are aligned properly (i.e., what Handy refers to as "best fit"). To me, this diagram displays the need for constant balance (or as discovered in the next section, "Skills," a constant shifting of the other six S's). For example, if all the categories are shifted to the left (tight and rigid), it would be difficult, if not impossible, for smooth operations to occur. Why? Because different people and different departments cannot hold separate tight and rigid beliefs in regard to business functions and expect cooperation and teamwork to happen spontaneously (and everybody carries their own beliefs and expectations concerning how tasks should be performed). However, common ground and flexibility must be willingly given at some point to avoid deadlocks (or worse) with co-workers. Tasks that demand rigid, serialized procedures will therefore require workers who will abandon their own rigidness to adapt to the task.

Likewise, neither could all the categories be aligned too far to the right (flexible), which could lead to anarchy. Again, proper balance needs to be obtained so that if the leader leans more to the right, subordinates must rely on self-discipline and self-control to keep things well in hand (and vice versa, or someone will be replaced). If the environment is extremely flexible, then a more rigid approach to operations should be adopted for competent and ethical organization to occur.

Theoretically, the closer to the center each category moves, the sturdier or more balanced the organization becomes. If one category shifts to the left or right (which can and will happen on a day-to-day basis), another must compensate in the opposite direction so that balance can be maintained. The better the balance or fit, the better the functioning of the organization.

Because Recreation Services was located in such a tight environment, our learned values in becoming and remaining flexible at the other levels enabled the changes that led transformation to take hold. "Best fit" shows the relationship and dependency of the other variables.

How can leaders, subordinates, tasks, and the environment be manipulated so that a "best fit" can result? "Hard minds" and "soft hearts" are terms Pascale (1991) uses to describe the contending opposite extremes of shared values. "Hard minds" pertains to bottom-line orientation while "soft-hearted" values reflect the intangibles that are tied to higher-order ideals affecting those in the company structure (e.g., dignity, respect, fairness, boldness, etc.). All businesses for solvency's sake must adhere to bottom-line results, but these must be balanced with soft-hearted values for the organization to "come alive." This forms the concept of excellence and total quality and brings about the drive and enthusiasm that separates different organizations. Maintaining this drive keeps one at the top.

Richard Pascale (1991), in a rousing example of understatement, suggests a way to remain on top and confront the numerous changes facing organizations:

> Staying in touch with what is really going on is the best way to force one's self to grow. The reason for being on the shop floor isn't to interfere, but to *get grounded*. Getting grounded is essential because it draws us into experience. If our experiences are far enough out of whack with our beliefs, we are forced to update our thinking. . . . too often we increasingly live in our perception of what's "right," "wrong," "impossible," etc., instead of in what is *real*. . . . The most gifted members of humanity are at their creative best when they cannot have their way. Creativity and adaptation are born of tension, passion, and conflict. Contention makes us whole and propels us along the journey of development. Limitations in the thinking of leadership are often the root cause of a company's demise. The tragedy of adult life is that we are much more likely to fulfill our perceptions about how the world works than we are to fulfill our goals, ideals, and visions. This shapes the destiny of our organizations (italics added)

(and ourselves). The story of Recreation Services provides overwhelming proof toward the truth of these words.

Skills

Skills are the distinctive capabilities of key personnel and the form as a whole. These are the things which the organization and its key personnel do particularly well—the capabilities that truly set a company apart from competition. The most significant aspect of skills is that it is the dependent variable. In other words, skills is a derivative of the other six S's. We must systematically fine tune the other six S's [i.e., "best fit"] to shift skills accordingly. (Pascale, 1991)

"The concept of a manager is usually seen in terms of a person who has more work than he or she can perform personally, and who arranges for some of this work to be carried out by others through delegation to subordinate staff. Management involves getting work done through the efforts of other people" (Mullins, 1992). Empowerment, delegation, and ownership of work at the Club did not occur overnight. A slow, methodical approach developed a staff that could run their own activities and programs. We were set apart from other recreation departments in that our employees almost literally ran the show (after the appropriate training), leaving me, as management, with the time to motivate, encourage, train, think, and pursue our facility improvement projects. Most of the other leisure managers in the city appeared to still be under the impression that their job was to tell the staff what to do. We operated by finding out what it was *customers* needed, exploring the resulting work that was required, and then letting everyone get on with it. Staff training was ongoing and became self-induced; because everyone was performing beyond what had been expected, the employees were encouraged to attend meetings, tournaments, and get-togethers around the city that pertained to their areas of expertise. These sessions were not only relaxing and enjoyable; they displayed an open trust in the staff and provided them with even more information and materials to think over in order to create and expand their activities.

The systematic reshuffling of the previous six S's established productive units able to focus on specific problems, and over two years, the following results were obtained. As this was the first time in eighteen years that so much was completed, the value of "we can make a difference" was cast.

AMENITIES CENTRE AND OFF-SITE GAME ROOMS

The Amenities Centre was the focal point of Recreation Services. It was where all staff offices were located, where program sign-ups took place, and where most of the Hospital-based facilities were located. This building was in a terrible state, and it took approximately eighteen months to have it partly refurbished. Approval would never have been granted to have this done all at once. A two-year period of using petty cash funds paid for the piecemeal repainting, recarpeting, furniture reupholstering, equipment repair, and numerous other improvements.

The staff was encouraged to choose the new colors, and the arts and crafts instructors painted a huge mural consisting of the Olympic sport symbols (of activities we offered) in bright colors on the main hall's wall. "Melba peach" and "Arizona sunset" (a light-reddish sand color) covered the remaining interior walls and added a modern and completely different feel to the building. All staff members were also encouraged to redo their offices in ways that they felt were the most suitable. This continuously brought home to everyone the physical and mental changes taking place within the organization. Other smaller off-site areas and rooms were spruced up much in the same fashion. Every employee was getting involved.

CHANGING ATTITUDES

Mental barriers are more difficult to break through than physical barriers. This posed a particular problem with the administration, who wanted change but did not wish to become involved or grant its authorization. Our first confrontation was with the executive committee board over a travel agent contracted to supply the airline tickets to employees (arranged as part of every Hospital employee's benefits), permitting employees one annual visit to their homes in other countries. A "gentleman's" agreement also implied that Recreation Services' sponsored trips must use this same agency. Many times the agency charged us over 50 percent more for its service than other travel companies, and the agency's service was terrible. Most of the board members and the chairman did not care. Although faced with mounting debt problems, some Saudis have grown up expecting money to be given rather than earned; such is the dilemma of an oil-rich country. Privately, an agreement was reached with the Club's assistant executive director to reduce the cost of our sponsored trips to our customers by going with the lowest bidder for group travel arrangements, relying on the apathetic nature of the board to ignore the fact that they had told us not to. It worked; we saved money and made money by passing the savings on to the customers.

Most of these attitudes against changing the status quo had developed over the years, and it was going to take time to dispel some of them. Slow, methodical change in a positive direction did more to change attitudes than outright, in-your-face confrontation (although there were times I mistakenly tried that route). Sometimes it is best to simply be more discreet or beg forgiveness than ask permission.

SPORTS COURTS

Consultation with our own tennis instructors and coaches provided a good idea of what was needed. All the courts required resurfacing, but because of the exceptionally hot Arabian sun, new surfacing needed to be chosen carefully. Several new tennis and multipurpose courts also had to be built. Since Hospital policy stated that any work over approximately $100,000 must go through a bidding process, I made certain that only top contractors submitted bids. This proved to be a "Keystone Cop" type of affair. Local law enabled the lowest bid from any business to be given the contract, and, with a public bid to be made, we did not want a disreputable company bidding. This had caused a number of problems in the past, as the lowest bid often resulted in shoddy workmanship and some of the lowest quality materials imaginable. Some companies making bids had no expertise in the specialties we required. Riyadh was filled with disreputable contractors; theoretically anyone could have made a bid. At one point, the Club's assistant executive director waited outside the chief executive director's office to intercept and explain the inherent problems with the public bid directive from the bids and contracts department. Much persuasion had convinced the Club's director that publicly announced bidding was the wrong procedure if a reputable contractor was wanted. He was able to convince the chief executive director of this despite much protest from the bids and contracts department. Only three contractors were permitted bids and a reputable construction company was obtained.

It took one year of persistence to develop this project to the bidding process. However, during this time, the Club's executive assistant director and myself were becoming closer allies, something that had not been the case earlier. Although he usually cast a weary eye upon our persistence, our intent was never questionable; progress was already being rapidly made on many fronts.

Once the court renovations were underway at the different sites, a few problems were encountered, most notably with the Engineering Department who mistakenly forgot to inform the contractors of the water pipes and electrical lines buried beneath the old court surfaces. There were a few ruptures from time to time that left the work areas literally flooded for days. Every security guard on duty did not seem to know what was going on despite the appropriate measures, forms, and paperwork being approved by the security department months earlier. But the bottom line is that for the first time in the department's history, the Hospital had a multitude of "new" courts.

EXERCISE GYM

Another year in the making, the new exercise gym was the first facility to be granted administrative approval. Not surprising, this verbal approval was then forgotten by almost everyone concerned. Although health clubs and fitness are very popular worldwide, there was no proper gym at the Hospital despite an enormous demand and much verbal insistence from many employees on obtaining one. A visit to all the major hotel fitness facilities in Riyadh proved that companies delivering exercise equipment to the Middle East (with its own unique problems, e.g., no companies with Jewish or Israeli customers or connections, etc.) were few and far between. Eventually a manufacturer in California was found. Unfortunately, we had to purchase all items from North America through a purchasing company established by the Hospital to prevent companies from increasing the price of their goods when the buyer was found to be from Saudi Arabia. This purchasing company proved to be full of crooks who ordered the gym equipment from the manufacturer and upon the completion of our custom-built exercise machines, threatened to go with another company unless a kickback was paid (according to the manufacturer's vice president).

This went on for some time while the equipment sat in storage in California. The manufacturer refused to comply. When the Saudi director of this American-based purchasing company made his annual visit to the Hospital, I arranged an appointment to try to work these problems out. It proved futile. During our forty-minute meeting, he never once looked up from the car magazine he was browsing through, and he accused me of having relatives in the manufacturer's company who "obviously would benefit from the sale."

After several more months of this type of runaround, I finally lost my temper. "Blazing" memos were written and affixed to copies of the manufacturer's letters, which detailed the purchasing company's discreetly hidden objectives. They were sent to anyone of authority. Numerous angry phone calls and meetings finally enabled me to purchase this equipment directly, an unprecedented procedure in the twenty-year history of the Hospital. This was allowed in part because it was argued that the Club had a separate budget that should require no more than Club executive committee approval for purchases. Sometime later, I was given a reprimand (the only one received in the two years) concerning large mirrors obtained for the gymnasium walls and paid for with a Club check (signed by all the necessary administrators). "Although you were given the authority to purchase these mirrors," the director of finance and accounting stated, "you were in no way given permission to pay for them." (?!?)

Resentment of the department's successes, the persistent methods used to achieve them, and the politics required to follow them through were beginning to show. During this time, appreciation letters from Hospital employees began to trickle in. This had never happened before, and the suspicious Club chairman angrily called me into his office to explain what was going on. He, in all sincerity, thought it was a trick.

Because so many people from many different departments were interested in the new gym, it was relatively easy to have it recarpeted, repainted, and have a new ceiling installed. Today this exercise gym is such a success that plans are being considered to knock down adjacent office walls in order to expand it further.

SQUASH COURTS

The Club only had a few squash courts. Nevertheless, they were often used. With the renovation of this area, after the fitness gym unpleasantness, a different approach was used. Many Executive Committee members had been coming down to Recreation Services to see the improvements that were being made, and I simply made sure that they were escorted into the squash courts before they left. One look at the peeling walls, damaged floors, and crumbling ceiling and a contractor was hired, with their blessing, within a few weeks. For many committee members, this was the first time they had seen the facilities in years, and many of them realized that the appalling conditions had not been exaggerations.

When the work was finished, hospital security guards tried to confiscate the contractor's equipment by claiming it belonged to the Hospital. This occurred despite the proper approvals, notifications, listings, and permits necessary for outside contract work. After two weeks of concerted efforts, the contractor's equipment was finally released. My worst fears were realized when the contractor politely informed us that they would not do any more work for us in the future. Unquestionably, they had the finest reputation in town.

TEXTURED SURFACE COVERINGS

Some of the pool deck surfaces had been covered with AstroTurf in order to protect bathers' feet from the baking hot sun and to provide a color and texture to break up the monotony of the ever pervasive look of concrete. Every few years, new AstroTurf of the lowest quality was purchased that tore, shed, and shred in less than one year. For the remaining years, the pools would look terrible until complaints became too loud, and the process for replacement would begin anew. The cost of this was very high, and common sense dictated that if a high quality, durable covering was put down, it would save the expense, time, and frustration of this draining cycle.

A supplier of stadium quality AstroTurf with a twelve-year guarantee was found, but the administration balked at the high price even though it was pointed out that the cost would be less than what we were paying in replacements. Despite the Hospital's main pool once being considered a showpiece and a much used venue for administrative functions, award ceremonies, and VIP dinners, this now disgraceful eyesore could not gain approval for renovation.

It took a year and a half and three proposals to finally get the approval, and two, but not all, of the needed locations were covered. A large wet/dry industrial vacuum was purchased to maintain these surfaces; pool furniture and heavy duty vandal-resistant umbrellas were later procured (only after the Club's chairman realized none were available to borrow for his private garden parties); and the pool areas were completely refurbished. They especially looked nice in the evenings when surrounded by torches, miniature lights, and decorated tables for dinner functions. These constituted the last of the big equipment purchases during the two years.

NEW PROGRAM DEVELOPMENT

Empowering the employees with the authority to make their own decisions had given them ownership of their work and with it the freedom to create new activities correlating directly with their own interests and specialties. The number and variety of the programs available soared. This included working together with outside businesses as much as possible. The department secretary suggested that we run our international trips in conjunction with another Hospital's recreation department. We were able to offer previously unheard of excursions to many exotic locations with much less work and preparation (although supplying different exit/entry visas to an international group always remained incredibly difficult). Trip cancellations were reduced to zero from 1992's 100 percent. We found out that Hospital employees did not want to travel abroad together, and by bringing in another Hospital's workforce and *lowering* the number of trips offered, we could increase the participants on these excursions, which always required a minimum number of participants to be viable. Local trips increased dramatically, with many having to utilize waiting lists. Tours and trips to factories proved the most successful—something the staff insisted that customers wanted and to which I remained so skeptical that it was almost overruled. Another among our achievements was the development of programs recognized as "firsts" in Riyadh or, indeed, the country itself.

Located less than one kilometer from the Hospital, a leading international hotel was building the world's first center-city golf course. This golf course was also only the second all-grass course in Saudi Arabia. Months before it opened, a professional golf manager was hired to oversee its construction and setup. I met this man at an embassy party and enthusiastically asked about corporate memberships. Although no thought had been given to the idea yet, he welcomed the concept. A carefully cultivated friendship developed, during which time the proposal of purchased memberships was cautiously given to the administration. As expected, it did not meet with approval by the Club's executive board who had never heard of golf and when it was explained, considered it a silly game of no interest or popularity. Two further attempts were also met unsuccessfully, until one evening the Hospital's chief executive director casually mentioned to one of the board members that a new golf course was opening nearby, and since many doctors liked to golf. . . .

Overnight the board's enthusiasm for this project erupted into a "quick action" scenario. Shortly thereafter a corporate membership arrangement allowing Hospital employees access to the golf course was established. This led to an even more successful group lesson program. We became the first hospital recreation department in the country to offer such activities to its employees, and the resulting attention turned many heads. This was the moment when almost all Hospital employees realized that changes had been taking place at Recreation Services, and there was a noticeable increase in customer appreciation and attention.

Our last major coup was the introduction of an equestrian pro-gram—again, a first for a hospital recreation department. For years I had been searching for riding stables where the horses were well cared for. In Saudi Arabia's throw-away society, this proved to be frustrating and fruitless. The staff had been making inquiries for over a year, knowing of my keen interest in the sport (it is one of the few recreation activities in which I partake), and eventually a pri-vate stable sold and slated for a Saudi Olympic training site, then sold again, was rumored to be reopening.

Its location was in the Diplomatic Quarter, an area of the city specifically reserved for embassies and diplomats' housing in order to keep the diplomats free of the religious fundamentalism. This relative "safe zone" was only a few miles from the Hospital and with one look at its immaculate grounds and well-vetted horses, it was clear that this was the right place for which we had been searching.

An Irish couple who ran the riding academy also managed five other private stables and were pushed to their limits with work. I offered to help exercise and train horses for them on a volunteer basis. Six hours a week was given freely in order to build trust and integrity with this couple. Having lived in Saudi for years, they had wearily learned to turn away many volunteers who lacked any riding skills, quickly disappeared, or worse, publicly bragged about being able to ride, which brought unwelcome attention from religious officials. (Although women are forbidden to ride, they comprise the majority of participants—high walls and discriminating advertising keep away prying eyes.)

After several months, the subject of a corporate membership was mentioned. The owners had never considered this idea before but remained interested, and we actually developed the arrangement together. Because this provided a new revenue area for them, we were given a substantial discount for our help, and the reaction from the Club was very receptive. In fact, this was the easiest procure-ment of funds encountered (most Muslims hold horses in high regard). This has been confirmed as one of the more popular pro-grams offered by Recreation Services, and it certainly was different from what had previously been offered.

MISCELLANEOUS

Several smaller programs were also initiated. Six sewing machines in excellent condition had been stored away and not touched since 1978. It only cost a few dollars to have them oiled, serviced, and set up in a new, expanded and redecorated arts and crafts room. By sheer coincidence, four of the staff had worked as dressmakers or tailors in their home countries and we set up several popular sewing activities. The newly created space could also be used for volunteer Brownie and Girl Scout meetings sponsored by employee dependents. Other outside groups inquired about and used these facilities. Recreation Services was again becoming an integral part of the community.

The achievements were a *combined team effort* that made use of the many diverse skills that comprised Recreation Services' staff. A feeling of involvement ensured every employee's respective input, and as progress was made, it inspired additional efforts that became a reminder of what could be aspired to and accomplished. The amount of pride shown by the staff can simply not be put into words.

Not surprising, the number of complaints from customers, who had previously been upset over the poor conditions of the facilities, rose during the renovation process. This time many of the complaints centered around the noise and inconvenience from the renovation work as well as the angry assumptions of what might occur in the future once these facilities began being used again. At times it felt as if there was no winning, but once it was over, virtually everything paid off handsomely.

Mistakes were also made. One of the biggest was the replacement of an interlocking tennis court surface on two of the courts, each of which had lasted beautifully for about twelve years. They needed replacement. Much to our bewilderment, the chemical composition of the interlocking grid system had changed ("improved," said the manufacturer) over the years, and the new grids proved unable to withstand the sun and heat of the region. By this time, I had finished my two-year contract and was living in London.

My replacement solved the problem by installing the interlocking grid surface on the walkways leading to and from the Amenities

Centre. The results, as shown to me in photographs, were beautiful. The two tennis courts where the interlocking grid surfacing was intended were resurfaced with a heat-resistent coating; also the mistake proved to be a blessing. The walkways no longer needed daily sweeping and the maintenance crew could now spend more time cleaning the actual facilities.

A look back at Pascale's seven S's in graphic form represents where Recreation Services began its transformational process and how it concluded two years later. It is important to note that although the change process was initiated, work is still required for progress to remain at this level and to improve the department even further. Much work remains to be done to create the kind of program that would be acceptable worldwide. The distance covered during the two years, however, is quite substantial.

	At the beginning	Two years later
Strategy	Too much planning or no planning at all.	Opportunistic, flexible, adaptive. Action oriented.
Structure	Management and staff set apart from each other.	All parties become integrated.
Systems	Little communication except by memo. Highly bureaucratic.	Employees effectively able to exchange information and ideas on site and face-to-face.
Style	Management by threat or command.	Motivation, empowerment, and delegation. Staff became more self-managed.
Staff	Timid, frightened, apathetic, complacent.	Self-confidence gained. Willing to try new things. Further skill development.
Shared Values	"Do enough to just get by."	Respect, dignity, pride from work ownership and results. "I can make a difference. I *want* to make a difference."
Skills	Held back.	Used to their full potential.

Change in Retrospect

Although most academic explanations begin by identifying a subject and exploring and building on its theories, here we end by viewing the theories after focusing on the case study because this is how the actual chain of events occurred. First, the transformation took place, and then I began to study how and why it was successful. Many documented successful change scenarios took place with no master plan. Management set out into the unknown with, as Richard Pascale has described, the heart of an explorer and the mind of a building contractor. To stop and reflect on where one began provides insight into future direction and can also create an incentive to continue further. Too much analysis is an anathema to change, but a basic understanding of its principle functions is important.

The following excerpt has been slightly adapted from *Management: Theory and Practice*, by Gerald Cole (1993) and presents the core of our subject well:

> To change something implies altering it, varying it, or modifying it in some way. Organizations change, or adapt, what they want to achieve and how. Some organizations change mainly in response to external circumstances (reactive change); others change principally because they have decided to change (proactive change). Some organizations are conservatives in outlook, seeking little in the way of change; others are entrepreneurial in outlook, ever seeking new opportunities and new challenges. Some organizations are so constructed (even constricted!) that change, i.e., adaptation, is a slow and difficult process; others are designed with built-in flexibility, enabling adaptation to take place regularly and relatively easily.
>
> Change does not always imply innovation, i.e., introducing something new, but it is this aspect of change that has attracted

the most attention from researchers. What are the key variables that have to be considered when looking at organizational change? They certainly include such fundamental variables as organizational structure, people, technology, and the external environment, but these in turn break down to include others such as decision-making processes, senior management commitment, organization mission and strategy, management style, employee motivation, communication systems, employee skills/know-how, and change agents (levers). In addition to these variables must be added other issues such as resistance to change, the social and political environment, and organizational culture. Clearly, any study of change and/or innovation is likely to be a complex undertaking. There is not much point in "change for change's sake," and most people need to be persuaded of the need to change. Some fear change. The reality is that every human grouping has forces within it which keep it together and provide it with stability, and yet others which provide it with a reason to change or adapt.

Kurt Lewin (1951) illustrated the dilemma neatly with his classic notion of "Force-field theory." This theory suggests that all behavior is the result of an equilibrium between two sets of opposing forces (what he calls "driving forces" and "restraining forces"). Driving forces push one way to bring about change; restraining forces push the other way in order to maintain the status quo.

Generally speaking, human beings tend to prefer to use driving forces to bring about change. They want to "win" by exerting pressure on those who oppose them, but, as Lewin's model suggests, the more one side pushes, the more the other resists, resulting in no change. The better way of overcoming resistance therefore is by focusing on the removal or at least weakening of the objections and fears of the resisting side. Thus, the initial policy should be not "How can we persuade them of *our* arguments for change?" but rather, "What are *their* objections/fears, and how can we deal with them?"

The Force-Field Theory

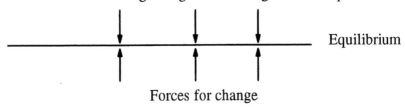

Forces resisting change/maintaining the status quo

Equilibrium

Forces for change

Lewin developed a three-stage approach to changing behavior that has been adapted and elaborated by Edgar Schein (1969) and comprises the following steps:

1. Unfreezing existing behavior (i.e., gaining acceptance for change)
2. Changing behavior (i.e., adopting new attitudes, modifying behavior)—usually requires a change agent
3. Refreezing new behavior (i.e., reinforcing new patterns of thinking/working)

"The unfreezing stage is aimed at getting people to see that change is not only necessary but desirable. The change stage is mainly a question of identifying what needs to be changed in people's attitudes, values, and actions, and then helping them to acquire ownership of the changes. The role of a change agent is crucial at this stage. The refreezing stage is aimed at consolidating and reinforcing the changed behavior by various support mechanisms (encouragement, promotion, participative management style, more consultation, etc.)" (Schein, 1969).

Paul Strebel is a professor of strategy and change management at IMD (Institute of Management Development) in Laussane, Switzerland. His 1996 research relays that,

> change may be constant but it is not always the same. Different types of change require different responses. The kind of situation in which restructuring makes sense is quite different from that in which experimentation might be appropriate. Thus, change leaders cannot afford the risk of blindly applying a

standard change recipe and hoping that it will work. Successful change takes place on a path that is appropriate to the
specific solution. . . . For example, managing a crisis in the
face of strong forces of change is completely different from
trying to stimulate change when everything is going well.
Moreover, stimulating change in an organization with low
resistance is not the same as trying to do so in the face of high
resistance. (Strebel, 1996)

Strebel has devised a model (simplified here) explaining con-
trasting change paths and their correlation with resistance and the
forces of change:

Type of Change

		Proactive	Reactive	Rapid
Resistance to Change	High	Radical Leader-ship (i.e., cha-risma)	Reassigning People and Responsibilities	Eliminating Jobs and/or People
	Medium	Management-Led Changes	Redesigning of Processes	Autonomous Restructuring
	Low	Employee-Led Changes	Goal Setting Creates Incen-tives to Make Changes	Rapid Adaptation to Change
		Weak	Moderate	Strong

**Perceived Need to Adopt Change
(Change Force)**

It is useful to distinguish between the different levels of
"change-force" intensity. Weak change forces are difficult to
discern and require skill in communications and in identifying
the value creating idea—but there is time for experimentation.
Moderate change forces are those which have started to affect
performance but do not threaten survival; getting people's
attention is easier and multidisciplinary teams should be employed.

Those organizations with high resistance have very few
"change agents" and require a radical approach to break the
dominant culture. The process should start with resistors at the
top, can benefit from headstrong leadership (though can equally

end in a disastrous ego trip), and requires some form of reorganization. In organizations that can be opened to change, management has to help the change agents, and top-down experimentation is desirable. In organizations that are already open to change, there is little risk in leaving the resistors until last. Bottom-up experimentation and goal cascading should be possible. (Strebel, 1996)

Many organizations are rethinking the way in which they do business to better serve their customers. The terms reengineering and restructuring are modern "buzzwords" used to explain the desire to focus on customers' needs and processes. These terms entail the reduction of customer waiting time, increasing product and service quality, the elimination of paperwork, and a general streamlining of all systems to better serve the customer (in its broadest sense). This involves rethinking the entire organization by cutting through formal departmental boundaries to foster creativity, innovation, free thinking, and increased production. It can also reduce costs. Both management and employees have an important role to play in this setup because action is necessary.

For management, listening, furnishing good training, and delegation provide the key to a productive employee relationship. Rewarding good performance is crucial, as is showing trust and openness and valuing the employee's work, ideas, and input. Creating a motivating environment conducive to creativity, participation, and innovation leads to problem solving full of variety and ingenuity. It also leads to being better prepared for change.

Employees need to understand that they must be willing to take and handle responsibility, that constant learning and training are a part of every job, and that the ownership of problems and solutions belongs to everyone in the organization. Simply performing bottom-line duties is not enough. Wages are given for value created. Be reminded that customers pay all salaries, and everyone's job becomes more pleasant and less stressful when everyone pulls in the same direction.

To me, the almost magical derivative of change is serendipity. For example, demanding that the staff become CPR certified was initially done for safety reasons, but the outcome presented a confidence and morale booster when employees were rewarded with certificates of accomplishment. Productivity increases resulted from delegation to subordinates in order to free up management's time to pursue other matters, and the establishment of an equestrian program began as a personal search for a riding stable. The renewal of our work sites and facilities transformed into a greater emphasis on work quality and quantity.

The term "change levers" is used to describe that which instigates the beginning of a change process. At Recreation Services, the pulling of these levers began with an almost emotional crusade to stop the degradation of the department and its people, and continued its passage through personal, organizational, and physical enhancements, conflict resolution, as well as individual and team integration, growth, and renewal. Some of the changes required rapid and strong change measures (Frank's termination, arranging for payment for the fitness equipment, dealing with customer complaints and abuses, etc.); others took moderate paths (changing the work areas, enhancing communication, building alliances, etc.), and some changes were "weak," (employee-led) (program enhancements, new activity ideas, reward systems, etc.).

> By keeping an eye on the evolving interplay between the forces and altering the change path accordingly, [organizations] can optimize their chances of success. Change is too uncertain to be predictable and once an organization starts out on a path, forces of change and resistance may respond in unexpected ways. Many change journeys involve more than one path. (Strebel, 1996)

The direction traveled by Recreation Services included several paths that, through the concerted efforts of a host of individuals, ended up as a journey which traveled the same direction.

Results

Changes brought about a host of improvements. The information used to make the following graphs and the quotes were taken directly from the Club's *Annual Financial Reports* and reflects the physical and mental improvements brought about during the two years of transformation:

> The Recreation Centre is one of the examples where sincere efforts have been made to inject new life into the recreational activities. Several new facilities were started and renovations made to the existing ones. The number of recreational activities as reported by the Centre has jumped to almost 1,400. . . . Revenue has also increased considerably. (First year)
>
> After closing a very successful year in the short history of the . . . Club, the staff started the new year in high spirits and with full confidence. In the early part of the year, activities within different domains of the. . . . Club were flourishing. Some areas, such as the Recreation Centre, took the lead and produced unprecedented results by providing a great variety of activities and fun to the. . . . Club members in particular and Hospital employees in general.
>
> The Recreation Centre took aggressive and dogmatic steps to enhance the existing recreation facilities by acquiring new equipment. Several renovation projects were also simultaneously undertaken to intensify its operations. The positive impact of these changes was very much visible, and several hundred more employees opted to become members of the . . . Club. (Second year)

Club Membership. Membership increased 34 percent—the largest recorded two-year gain.

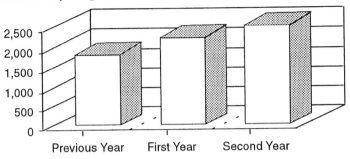

Membership Revenues (In Saudi Riyals). Revenues increased 35 percent—again, the largest recorded two-year gain.

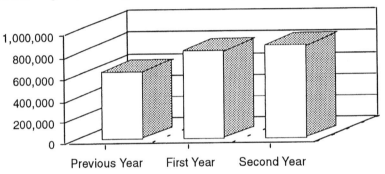

Club Net Profit (In Saudi Riyals). These were the largest net profits in the Club's history.

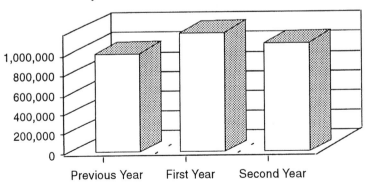

The increase of net profits by 55 percent during the first year was the largest single annual gain ever made. Profits decreased slightly the following year (3 percent) because of the over 1,300,000 Saudi Riyals that were spent on the purchases, renovations, improvements, and construction projects previously mentioned. The Club's recorded gross revenues reached approximately $2.25 million at their highest. Recreation Services has still not become self-financing. However, through conversations with the current management, the situation has improved and continues to improve considerably.

Recreation Activities, Programs, and Trips

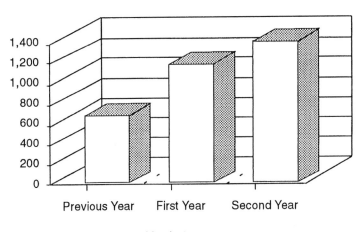

Yearly Averages

The graph above is perhaps the most important. In essence, it shows the productivity increases that occurred over the two-year period. Productivity increased 82 percent, an unprecedented result. During this period, no other recreation department in Saudi Arabia was found that could match or improve on these statistics. Larger departments around the country with greater workforces apparently cannot achieve similar outcomes. Even after I left, activities, programs, and trips have continued to increase. There still has not been a single department found in the country that can match these figures. Employee empowerment has proven to be a resounding success and continues to bring about a program that exceeds all expectations.

With these results come the almost inevitable increases in revenues and profits.

International trip cancellations decreased to 0 percent the first year and were maintained at 0 percent throughout the second.

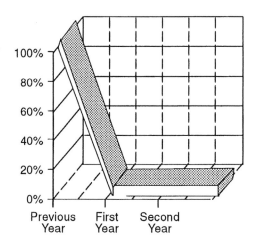

At the twelve recreation sites located around the city and within the department itself, the following results were achieved during the two-year transformational time period:

- Renovation of five tennis courts
- New construction of two tennis courts and two basketball/multipurpose courts
- Creation of a new modernized fitness facility
- Formation of a new arts and crafts room
- Many building interiors painted and recarpeted
- Renovation of the squash courts
- Complete renovation of the main recreation facility's pool deck
- Improvements and additions to other residential exercise/fitness facilities
- Construction of two new volleyball courts
- Improvements to all work areas and offices
- Renovation of residential community facilities (meeting halls)
- Development of new programs and activities

- International trips successfully merged with another local hospital's recreation department
- Improved staff morale and productivity
- Large increases in the number of exhibitions and displays
- Reduced program cancellations
- Restocked supplies and equipment with inventory system setup
- Purchase and use of a new computer
- Enhanced monthly "Recreation Bulletin"
- Replacement of broken furniture and equipment
- New cleaning standards set for all facilities
- Pay raises for deserving staff members
- Disposal of unsafe equipment, chemicals, and broken items.

During this time, improvements were made at other areas subordinate to Recreation Services as well:

- The beauty shop was renovated and expanded considerably.
- The barber shop was upgraded and moved to a new and modernized location.
- Child Care Services underwent numerous improvements, such as the purchase of new toys (something which had not been done in years) and renovations, including the hiring of a wonderful new supervisor.

Case Study Conclusions

Initiating change is a gut-wrenching experience. People almost always try to resist change. Throughout the writing of this case study, a number of books and articles were read concerning organizational transformations, and all of them involved enormously emotional and frustrating processes. Change does not come easily. A crisis is usually, although not always, the instigator.

The Nike athletic wear company states it well in their advertising: "There is no finish line." Transformation is an ongoing process. It demands that we look at ourselves, our organizations, where we are headed, and where we want to go. It takes us through triumphs, setbacks, mistakes, and corrections. It humbles and gives confidence. But most important, it provides sources of inner growth and learning that never end—provided we take the journey by deciding not to remain inactive.

I have found that in a service-based industry, many reasons for initiating change are highly relevant. Decentralization, the process that moves decision making from the management hierarchy's "center" to those "on the front line," is especially important. In the service profession, it is crucial to give customers answers on the spot. Who else is best suited to provide these responses other than those who deal directly with customers? Empowerment and delegation are vital components. Not only do these standards provide an opportunity for the workforce to prove themselves, they can generate an involvement in work previously unknown. Most people will put more effort into that which they can call their own, and this includes the organization. Providing work ownership can build strong customer relations with employees and result in dramatic increases in productivity. Proper training facilitates the essential developments.

Teams and teamwork are the keys to problem solving, and successful teamwork can free up enormous amounts of time for management to pursue other concerns. Teams often set high standards and can provide necessary inner competition and positive tensions. They also can work quickly. Teams can get everyone involved to work and tend to weed out any slackers. Few things can bring an organization together as quickly as an evolving team-based strategy, and fewer things help us to stay in touch with reality and stay grounded.

Dealing with a variety of conflicts is part of any management role. How we view conflict determines its outcome because conflicts are inevitable and do not always translate into fistfights. "Disagreement among people in relationships, groups, and organizations comes with the territory" (Kindler, 1988). Learning how to handle (or create) conflict effectively, then using it wisely, can produce dividends. What one person sees as a "wall," another may perceive as an opportunity. Achieving *functional* conflict is not easy and there is no set plan. Different situations demand different strategies. Experience can teach us how to tap into this plethora of energy. The complete elimination of conflict may lead to complacency and stagnation.

Communication is the common thread running through all these theories. Secrecy only creates dissension, while an open and honest exchange of information reduces many anxieties and frustrations. Effective communication plays an integral role in solving problems, setting and meeting work standards, improving customer and employee relations, and providing staff recognition and rewards.

Breadth and depth of change is required for transformation to take hold. It is important to involve as many people as possible in the change process. This ties together teamwork, communication, work ownership, empowerment, and decentralization. Creating commitment to an inspiring vision demands total involvement; total quality is the result.

Strong leadership is a necessity. Leaders or "heroes" (as some management books call them) can appear anywhere up or down the organizational framework. It is significant that there are those whom others can rally around and who provide *vision, comfort, direction,* and *security.*

Risk taking is essential. Too much discussing, analyzing, and waiting for just the right moment can be anathema. Omelets cannot be made without breaking a few eggs. Change occurs slowly, and any progress must be interpreted *as progress* despite any setbacks. Whenever anything new is being tried, someone somewhere along the line will have to stick his or her neck out.

Finally, as mentioned throughout the second section of the book, persistence and consistency cannot be overstated.

And what of Recreation Services? Will these changes hold? Only time will tell. Unfortunately, the department is surrounded by an asphyxiating bureaucracy that seems to reward complacency, and the country itself is faced by a growing religious fundamentalism. If the staff are allowed to continue tackling their own problems and concerns, their chances of survival are good. Continued success (especially in being considered leaders in the Riyadh recreation community) will help, but without a maverick to rally behind and buck the system from time to time, however, they may lose some ground.

One of the major problems now faced by Recreation Services is one that I created. Not thinking far enough ahead was the cause. Improving the organization and its facilities has generated such an increase in use that the larger customer base has brought a myriad of new problems and grievances. Hospital statistics show that the over 5,000 employees and dependents now use recreation programs and facilities so often that it appears as if 15,000 people are being serviced. Sincere efforts are underway to meet this increasing demand, now that we have shown that we are worth the investment. Still, the transformation process has a long way to go and must be continued for any future challenges to be met successfully. The gains made, however, work substantially in the department's favor.

For Recreation Services, adaptability, persistence, inner growth, and teamwork provided the components needed to meet the inevitable forces of change and created a success story that business authors have been writing about for years. When will others get the message?

Recreation Services Today

Because of the numerous successes Recreation Services was able to achieve, the department has proven itself in the eyes of the previously skeptical Hospital and Club administrations. Six new cleaning staff have now been added, as well as three recreation specialists and a security guard.

A new manager from the United States arrived some time ago and is now the new coordinator (head of recreation). In a short time, approval has been granted to renovate more facilities. The speed of this is almost unbelievable, especially since this man has been introduced to the all-pervasive bureaucracy for just a short time. He has relayed his astonishment at the unfriendliness and outright rudeness of many of the Hospital's staff he now services and has commented that, "Everyone seems to have my telephone number and they call me at every hour of the day or night. Most of these people have serious emotional problems, not recreation problems." Some things never change.

Interestingly, this new manager insists he hears nothing but compliments about the department's turnaround. Many customers and staff have relayed stories about the "miracle" that occurred between 1993 and 1995. No doubt these comments may come from those who once took great pleasure in ridiculing Recreation Services and now wax nostalgic about "the good old days."

The number of programs, trips, and activities continues to climb. The staff's training has been thorough and the new coordinator has commented on this as well as the employees' ability to keep him well informed about what is going on, recreation-wise, in Riyadh. "It's as if I have lived here for years," he said. One day, he stated over the telephone that a citywide recreation league organization, comprised of members and managers from other recreation departments, is now asking him for advice as to how they can achieve similar results.

Despite the popularity of the equestrian program, it will probably be discontinued due to a more than doubling of the membership fees. The golf program is also facing problems. The International Hotel Golf Club has changed its rules, policies, and golf managers so many times that customers have been avoiding many activities. This was due to an in-house power struggle between the Hotel's sales and marketing department and its golf course management. In the process, the Golf Club has lost a great deal of community respect and, of course, customers.

A year after I left, a terrorist bomb attack, less than a kilometer from the Hospital, caused a two-week cancellation of all trips and activities outside the Hospital's boundaries. Numerous correspondence from friends still employed at the Hospital tells of the dire financial straits now seriously affecting all operations. The Hospital's maintenance department, for example, has been almost completely disbanded, and it is extremely difficult to purchase goods now, as many of the suppliers have not been paid for some time and word has spread that the Hospital does not honor its debts. It seems the negative external influences, outside the Club's control, continue unabated.

It is hoped that improvements will continue to be made despite these and other setbacks, and it appears that this is exactly what is happening. Both the recreation staff and the department have proven their abundant capabilities in the past, despite mounting problems. Provided they are allowed the opportunities to do so, there is no reason why they should not remain leaders in their field. Certainly by now they know what can be accomplished.

PART III: COMPONENTS

Introduction

In Part III, a different tone and approach is taken. Having looked at an organization and its workings through a transformational case study, let us now examine the practices of good business in general. These components constitute a closer look at what has, in a lesser context, already been touched upon (within a much different format) in the previous section. The topics discussed in this section are the components of successful leisure business operations. They represent what I feel are the most important areas in leisure business and the areas that need constant attention from both management and nonmanagement staff. Since the leisure industry is service-based and thrives on people, it should be no surprise that most of the components of leisure businesses are people oriented. Much attention needs to be focused on employees and customers and effective communication with, and between, the two. The following essays, and their examples (from a wide variety of experiences), present and discuss some of the most important aspects of good leisure business operations. When business is not going well, investigating and then successfully changing one or more of these subject areas will usually correct any problems.

Understanding Good Customer (or Guest) Service

Much of the change necessary in a leisure-based business involves enhancing or improving customer service. Few things are as important to a leisure business as the services provided for customers or guests. This is especially true in the leisure industry, which is heavily service oriented. Customers are the lifeblood of every business organization because the essence of every business is to attract and retain customers. Without customers, there would be no jobs or paychecks, no matter how wonderful the product. Just as important, customers are not easy to come by and must be carefully cultivated. Responding to customers' needs is of paramount importance and every employee needs to set this as a priority.

What are the needs of customers and guests? The answer is simple: ASK THEM. The Sedona Health Spa, a resort in Sedona, Arizona, spent several thousand dollars (mostly in start-up costs) utilizing questionnaires, letters, labor, and marketing techniques so they could find out just what their customers wanted in terms of programs and facilities. The result? Revenues increased $1,500 per month, staff talents were more fully utilized, and most important, clients loved the quality and diversity of the new setup. Results were so successful that plans are being made to continue polling customers on a monthly basis. The organization was able to reap these benefits by properly meeting customer needs (Powers and Short, 1996).

Customers are the individuals whom organizations serve. In its broadest sense, this includes *everyone* who we come into contact with at work. Look carefully at this definition, because not only does it involve those whose money we take in exchange for products or services, but also those people who have a relationship with the business both within and outside the workplace, including secretaries, co-workers, people from other departments, suppliers, contractors, and so forth. Being able to provide good customer care results in more secure and enjoyable work and increased revenues.

Employees who know of their importance to their organization and who fully appreciate their responsibilities within it have the ability to provide good customer service. Customer care emanates best from employees who feel that they are part of a team, that management cares for them, and that managers and others set a good example. It is also necessary that the needs of the staff, both as individuals and as a group, be regarded with equal importance and are fully related to achieving any work-related tasks. Thorough training and feedback should be ongoing requirements.

Proper training is an essential part of every employee's job, but it can be diminished through overregulation, rules, and procedures. The lion's share of interpersonal customer relations cannot be taught through robotics, assembly line processes, or learned in front of a chalkboard. It must be practiced. More often than not, good service is spontaneous, "unpackaged" assistance in which the customer feels unique. This is achieved through simple friendliness, common courtesy, and the willingness to provide honest and direct assistance in accordance with what the customer wants.

Several years ago, a large retail corporation renowned for its good service was researched in order to compare its service operations against that of a major competitor. The competitor was not doing well, and a look through its employee manual (the size of a large telephone book) showed page after page of procedures and regulations regarding their views on the proper way to act during work. The retailer who was excelling took a different approach. "We expect you to use your good judgment and common sense in all transactions" is their simple rule and forms their complete guide to customer care.

Good customer service begins with good ethics and includes truthful advertising, good phone etiquette, prompt and professional written correspondence, and *giving immediate attention*. It involves the parking lot, reception areas, and every facility throughout the premises. The whole team—managers, staff members, attendants, maintenance crews, cleaners, contractors, and employees—is ultimately responsible for creating a positive image. *No one is too busy to help*. Cooperation facilitates implementation at every level. Showing concern by responding quickly and in a friendly manner to the customer's presence, problems, and queries is the key. Eye contact, listening, remaining calm, and sounding cheerful are the components. Proper appearance and attitude is equally significant and essential. Knowing your organization and the people within it will enable answers to be found quickly and courteously when they are needed, particularly if that answer is "no" (which it should rarely be).

Perhaps one of the best examples of the importance of customers and their care was written by Graham Brooks, Managing Director of Dowman Car and Trucks, in Stockport, England. It has been adapted for use here:

- Customers are the most important people in our business.
- Customers are not dependent on us—we are dependent on them.
- Customers are not to argue or match wits with.
- Customers bring us their needs—it is our job to fill those needs.
- Customers are not an interruption of work—they are the purpose of it.
- Customers do us a favor when they call—we do not do them a favor by serving them.
- Customers are part of our business—they are not outsiders.
- Customers are deserving of the most courteous and attentive treatment we can give them.
- Customers are the individuals who make it possible to pay our wages.
- Customers are the lifeblood of this and every other business.

Make no mistake. If customers are not happy with the service given, they will take their business elsewhere. Although this information is certainly basic, if you think back upon the times that you have been put off by rudeness, glued-on grins, repetitive unhappy responses, or a general uncaring or patronizing manner, it becomes apparent that everyone, from time to time, is in need of a gentle reminder concerning the importance of good customer service. A full appreciation of this only helps us to provide the type of success, service excellence, and reputation we would all like ourselves and our organizations to have.

Difficult Customers

During the summer of 1989, I was working a part-time position supervising the leisure area of a beautiful hotel and convention center. The hotel had just spent a small fortune refurbishing the recreation facilities and was understandably quite keen to keep them in top condition. Dark-soled shoes and unsupervised children with food, for example, were not allowed on the new oak wood racquetball or squash floors, and so I nicely asked three children who fit this description to leave the courts.

Within ten minutes, I was confronted by a large man the size of a rugby player, red-faced with anger. Through clenched teeth he demanded to know if the facilities were for guest use. I gulped and calmly told him that yes, they indeed were; however, there were guidelines pertaining to appropriate attire, unsupervised children, and the eating of foodstuffs. With a rising voice that eventually reached shouting level, the giant bellowed that as guests of the hotel, he and his children were free to do as they pleased. In fact, he continued, his children would be on the courts first thing in the morning wearing and eating whatever they wanted. His children smirked at me as they stood behind their father licking their ice cream cones. I politely and calmly informed him that his children, as with any guest, were free to use the facilities by presenting a room key and that any damages would be charged to his account. That statement, of course, only added to his fury.

I have remembered this incident many times, not only because of the fear and embarrassment it caused, but also because of its outcome. The man and his children had been wrong in their actions. However, it took some time to realize that I had been wrong as well, very wrong, for I had been playing the unnecessary and dangerous game of one-upmanship. Besides, they never showed up the following day.

Many years ago, my mother was working in a large department store when an unkempt and wide-eyed woman approached the register. Pulling out an immaculate new bedspread still marked with its package-induced creases, the woman proceeded to thrust it continuously at my mother demanding a refund. When asked why she wanted her money back, the woman hysterically gestured and raised her voice, "Because it's covered with WORMS. CAN'T YOU SEE THEM?" An awkward silence amid open-jawed bewilderment set over Mom. Quickly regaining her composure, she agreed fully with the customer's complaints and hurriedly filled out a refund form, happily relieved that she was not working in the power tool section that evening. The situation had been well handled.

Regardless of where one works, if it involves dealing with customers, then it involves dealing with difficult customers. It is inevitable. Sooner or later, every organization must face the arrival of a customer who demands the impossible, wants to make a scene, feels the need to assert some form of authority, or needs to find some way to vent frustration or insecurity on an employee(s). As awkward as it is to discuss or even admit, everyone in the leisure profession has at one time or another witnessed or been subject to customer inconsideration, whether it be verbal harassment in front of colleagues or the seemingly innate ability some people have to create extraordinary messes or shun responsibility while on holiday.

The fact is, we rely on these customers and the money they spend to supply the business upon which our jobs and wages rely. It is almost always necessary to retain customers' business and your dignity when such problems arise, despite the raised voices and outright anger that so often accompanies these situations. Although no general prescription can be applied across the board (every situation is different), it is possible to apply a few principles that can diffuse many sticky customer situations:

- *Listen to the Customer.* Do not just let the customer talk, really listen. The customer may have a valid point and is just presenting it inappropriately. Try not to interrupt, and if the complaint is not too loud, let the customer continue to run out of steam. Do not trivialize the problem.
- *Remain Calm and Pleasant.* Speak softly and directly. Do not add fuel to the customer's fire by becoming excited, matching wits, or trying to get the upper hand. Control the situation by

controlling yourself. It is very difficult for irate customers to play their "game" when the opposition refuses to play.

- *Do Not Take any Remarks or Behavior Personally.* Try to get to the heart of the matter by leaving personalities or traits out of the picture. If you maintain your professionalism, you will not lose dignity, and you *will* look very good in the eyes of others. You will also have a good laugh about it sometime *later* in the employee lounge.
- *Solve the Problem* or at least make the attempt. Get a supervisor if one is needed or contact someone who can help. Do not pass the buck by sending the customer on a wild goose chase. Your goal is to solve the problem quickly and directly. Remember that customers often do not know your organization's setup and may be frustrated because they simply do not know where to turn for help.
- *Apologize and Thank the Customer* for bringing the matter to your attention. Even if you did not cause the problem. Acknowledgment is a powerful tool for disarming aggression.

Of course, there are times and situations that defy even the most resolute attributes of professionalism. One example is of a resort that catered a business convention which turned into a fiasco from the antics of a drunken executive who only became more incensed from the efforts of hotel employees trying to restore calm. During the episode, hotel employees were verbally and physically assaulted and monetary damage was caused. Faced with the loss of dignity from employees who had behaved admirably and damages that they did not wish to cover, hotel administration decided to confront the visiting executive the following morning. No amount of careful discussion would placate the individual, who only became more obstinate.

Not wanting to pursue the lengthy mess of legal action, hotel administrators followed a more clever course. The perpetrator's chief executive officer was contacted by telephone by the hotel's senior manager. Shortly thereafter, an apology and personal check arrived in the mail from the embarrassed and deservedly humiliated executive. The hotel had sent out a powerful message that reflected a desire to remain in control of its business and maintain its reputation for good service to both customers and employees.

Taking drastic action is not always warranted or possible. Mike was the manager of a chain of recreation facilities located in a midsized city. One morning, three maintenance men telephoned to report that they had caught a thirteen-year-old boy who had just pulled down a brand-new, canvas-covered structure designed to provide shade at one of the swimming pool locations. The boy had been caught swinging from this structure earlier but had continued his vandalism once the maintenance crew had resumed work.

Mike's operation was in a desert region, and with summer just around the corner, there was little time or money to repair the damage. Customers would have no shade, and Mike winced at the loss of business and inevitable complaints the organization would face. After visiting the destruction site and collecting as many facts as possible, the boy's parents were phoned later in the day. By then the child had found plenty of time to concoct a well-rehearsed lie. Imagine Mike's surprise when the mother berated him and threatened legal action for publicly grabbing and harassing her child and reducing him to tears. Mike had not even seen or spoken with the child. Fed up with the damage created by the children of "not my child" parents, Mike made the decision to follow through with the restitution of property by the boy's family.

After a week of unpleasantness that this action caused, Mike's superiors eventually decided to let the matter go. It would prove far easier to just cut the business's losses and move on. It was a difficult decision, and for Mike's organization, it was probably the right one. Sometimes (though not always), it is better to do all that is possible until a point is reached when what is sought becomes more expensive and energy consuming than the problem itself. This is often a decision that should be made collectively. That way everyone understands the reasons why it was made.

Prevention is probably the most effective way to deal with difficult customers. If the boy in the previous example had been escorted from the premises immediately upon being seen as unsupervised, the majority of the problems encountered would never have developed. Learning to anticipate problems can greatly diminish many incidents. This is the type of skill that any well-trained employee can develop, as is the handling of difficult customers. The importance of good customer relations can never be overstated, and it is essential to know where your business draws the line when it comes to difficult customers, particularly in cases where employees are in the right and need support.

Several months ago, I heard about the president of a software and electronics company who was proud, and justifiably so, of the complete and successful turnaround he had generated within his organization. He became famous (or infamous) for crediting good customer service for the company's success by demanding and expecting that employees always go the extra mile to satisfy customer needs. Customers had soon realized this, and the practice was responsible for creating an enormous amount of sales and business improvements.

However, it also sometimes drew employees to wit's end in providing for these needs. One group of overseas customers began making so many demands that the team assigned to handle them eventually phoned the company president saying that they had reached their limit. After some deliberation, the president decided to put his beliefs into action and lead by example. He flew to the location and personally supervised its operation.

After a full day or so of meeting rather exorbitant and bizarre customer demands, the president's patience began to grow thin. The following morning, the customers demanded that doughnuts be served before the day's activities began. The president swallowed his pride and went to purchase a platter full of doughnuts from the first market he could find that was open. When he returned, to his astonishment, the customers grew angry and started to complain because of what was presented; there were no jelly doughnuts. "If anyone wants to know where I draw the line at customer service," the beleaguered president later publicly admitted, "that's it."

Getting the Most from Employees

If customers are the lifeblood of business, then employees are its brain and muscle. Employees are the people who carry out the activities that make up an organization. They are the people who determine and create the direction the company goes and the people who deal with its customers. Employees include each and every person in the organization. From the chairman to the floor sweeper and everyone in between, all are and should be considered employees.

In *Top Performance* (1986), author Zig Ziglar designed a distinct way of looking at the modern organization that reflects the proper chain of command setup for customer-driven businesses and dramatically illustrates the importance of employees. Most of us are familiar with the typical pyramid-shaped hierarchical structure showing the labor force at the bottom and management at the top. Unfortunately, this is often interpreted as implying that those at the top are the most important. Here is a modification of Mr. Ziglar's organizational chart:

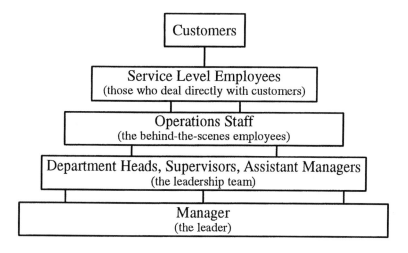

Viewing a pyramid-shaped, organizational chart from this perspective graphically shows the importance of the often disregarded customer-level employee in a business structure. In terms of who works for whom, the example suggests that the group on the bottom focuses on providing for the group at the top. Every employee inside the framework shares a common purpose: to work together to satisfy the customer (who should be determining true policies and directives).

With a full appreciation of this model and its structure comes the realization that the security, emotions, and well-being of employees do have an effect on the service that is given to customers. It therefore makes sense to ensure that employees are happy, well-trained, and able to deal with customers as effectively and efficiently as possible. Unfortunately, despite the impressive results gained by businesses all over the world that depend on this common sense "theory" for their success, many organizations have still not gotten the message.

From the examples that appeared in the previous Theories and Applications section, as well as numerous other case studies throughout the world, there is overwhelming evidence to show that one of the better ways to achieve satisfied and motivated employees is with "empowerment." Although the word may be new, the concept of empowerment is probably as old as time: *people are motivated for their own reason, not your reasons.* (Ideas cannot be implemented unless the people who *must* work with them *will* work with them.) Thus, it is dependent on the organization to provide incentives for self-motivation.

Ages ago, this could be accomplished with the use of fear or torture. Nowadays this means giving employees the power of controlling their own self-worth and, to some degree, controlling their own destinies through autonomous decision making and recognized input. Trusting employees by utilizing empowerment releases the talent, skills, and drive that can meet the constant changes which affect today's businesses. Only a crisis or exceptionally serious situation warrants a ruler-subject scenario.

The development and action toward an enlightened workplace does not happen overnight. You cannot simply wake up one morning and decide to instill the concepts of empowerment throughout a workforce. You must wake up *every* morning and do so. Empowerment requires groundwork. In effect, what is needed is a foundation. The building of this foundation demands that:

- information to make correct decisions is readily available to everyone;
- proper training and guidelines are given to instill a sense of direction and purpose;
- employees are trusted to manage themselves and their workgroups (teams); and
- supervisors will keep their distance and yet not ignore continuing results.

Guidelines are a prerequisite and are established to explain the basic expectations required from all employees.

For nonmanagers this includes:

- learning to take and handle responsibility;
- realizing that constant learning and training are a part of every job;
- understanding that the ownership of problems and solutions belongs to everyone in the business (problem prevention);
- knowing everyone needs to pull in the same direction;
- acting on the fact that showing up for work and performing bottom-line duties are not enough—wages are given for value created; and
- displaying caring, integrity, and trust.

For managers, this means:

- viewing workers as assets (not expenditures) and recognizing their value;
- sharing information and providing good training;
- listening, asking, valuing, and then acting on others' viewpoints and ideas;
- creating a motivating environment conducive to creativity, participation, and innovation;

- working toward preventing problems, not just battling them;
- rewarding good performance;
- displaying caring, integrity, and trust; and
- prudently choosing the right people for the right jobs.

Accomplishing the uppermost level in employee achievement is a full-time leadership job. One way to accomplish this is to involve employees in every process as much as possible. Care is needed to ensure that the tasks decided upon are challenging and achievable. The determination of just how much each employee can cope with, without any resulting boredom or frustration, should be done on an individual basis.

When reaching toward this objective, some individuals may not understand where to draw the line at friendship and subordination or leadership. Having or being the type of manager who is "soft" or one who is determined to be everybody's friend does not establish a challenging environment conducive to employees pushing themselves to discover their true capabilities. Neither is the type of atmosphere where management "manages" with bullying and fear tactics. These two extremes can be avoided by clearly:

1. establishing a set of definite goals, objectives, and priorities;
2. defining the guidelines and limitations in achieving these goals;
3. determining and establishing the methods to acquire these goals (with the employees' input); and
4. fairly evaluating progress and outcomes.

It is possible to unleash the forces of empowerment in almost any workplace. Remember that employee relations are a two-way street. Keep both lanes of communication open and keep in perspective that none of this incorporates completely letting go.

Evaluation of employee performance is vital and should be done on a consistent basis. Those who hire or supervise are obliged to let subordinates regularly know how they are doing. How else can employees learn if they are going in the right direction or are doing what is expected? Work evaluation takes into consideration the employees':

- overall job performance,
- work output and quality,

- colleagues' views (some companies take team members or colleagues' comments into consideration),
- social skills,
- attitude toward work and co-workers,
- punctuality and attendance, and
- views of who is being evaluated.

Evaluations should avoid: judgment on one trait (good or bad) to give an overall assessment, ignoring past performance and only judging recent work standards (which keeps the "evaluatee" from pouring on the goods right before evaluation time), personal bias, grading, or marking everyone as average.

Money is not always the motivational factor. If it were, there would be no such thing as volunteering. For many employees, motivation and cooperation are encouraged when they perceive their relationship in regard to the whole organizational picture and fully understand their value to it. In an environment where work relationships are friendly and professional, where rewards and incentives are regularly given, where leadership provides direction and vision, where face-to-face communication is encouraged, and where ideas and innovation are acted upon, productivity increases; operational cost reductions cannot be far behind.

Teamwork and Delegation

Teamwork and delegation may at first appear to be unrelated, but the two go hand in hand. Anyone who has ever participated in team sports or activities understands the importance of groups effectively working together to accomplish a goal, as well as the need for the common direction this goal requires. But, how many of us apply this concept in our workplace? How much time and energy is wasted in your organization playing politics, fighting over turf, bickering, sulking, and in essence, canceling each other out? Developing teamwork and applying delegation are two areas where successful implementation can lead to surprising breakthroughs in productivity.

Teamwork is more than just individuals working together to complete an objective. It also implies that departments and other units within and outside the business are working in unison and pulling in the same direction. Teamwork occurs when everyone involved completely takes part in and understands their organization's mission and objectives and their role in achieving these goals.

It is a good thing to remind ourselves from time to time that personal interests need to be placed on the back burner when the well-being of the organization suffers adversely. I have witnessed, in utter astonishment, the complete destruction of an enormously successful hotel golf course operation following an in-house power struggle between the golf club's management and the hotel's sales and marketing department. Despite the fact that none of the marketing and sales people had ever golfed before, they somehow won the fight. Politically, they won the battle by gaining control of the golf operation. But realistically, since the business was ruined by a group of people with unchecked ambitions who did not know what they were doing, everyone in the organization eventually lost.

Let us face it. If there are fifty people in a workplace, there is the potential for fifty differences of opinion. Organizations must learn how to handle these differences or the end result could be similar to the aforementioned golf business. Handling employee disagreement (or departmental disagreement) is not easy. People who feel passionately or emotionally for or against policies or decisions should be dealt with as difficult customers. Ultimately, strong leadership (which was sorely lacking at the golf club) is required to end confrontation.

Administration, marketing, finance, and operations are integral parts of a complete system that must be balanced to maintain smooth-running leisure operations Whether these components are comprised of one individual or complete departments, they are merely the vehicles used to produce quality services or products. Just as one horse cannot function with several riders giving different directions, so must a team operate with one leader and a willing and cooperative crew united in a common pursuit.

In any diverse leisure business, delegation is necessary simply because of the number and variety of activities offered. Empowering individuals or teams with the responsibility to create, develop, and follow through with recreational programs not only displays trust and respect on behalf of management, it is also a good way to expand and utilize employee talents, abilities, and confidence. Almost always, those who have been given the opportunity to prove their worth will pleasantly surprise themselves, management, and customers with a job well done. When delegation is seen as part of continuous training and not abdication, a relay of open communication between the parties concerned will facilitate successful operation. Inherent risks involved in decision making and program setup are then greatly reduced.

Despite the proliferation of material available today espousing the virtues of employee entrustment, managers sometimes find it difficult to delegate authority because of personal insecurity or a lack of trust in their staff. This is a shame. If the right people are initially chosen, then properly trained, and a clear explanation of objectives is presented, it only makes sense to use these people to their full ability. Ironically, it then makes the manager's job that much easier as well. Remember though, that this is not as easy to do as it is to say. Building trust and confidence cannot be accomplished overnight. It takes a great deal of time and patience, and all parties must be willing.

With the advent of teamwork and delegation, it is common for human conflict to arise from time to time. In business school, we are taught that conflict does not necessarily always translate into fistfights. In many instances, constructive conflict is considered healthy and invigorating, and many companies actually welcome it. However, there are distinct types of conflict, and the differences between them are enormous.

With *dysfunctional* conflict, issues are seen as being black or white, right or wrong. We either avoid or sadistically prepare for the imminent confrontation of those with opposing views. Meeting an opposite viewpoint is perceived as a battle to be won at all costs.

Constructive conflict respects opposing views and helps clear the air by introducing new ideas and innovations through the emphasizing of the importance of individual input and creativity. Mutual respect and a common purpose help shape these ideas so that the team can achieve the completion of their organization's objectives. In the leisure industry, where we deal primarily with people, learning to successfully handle conflict is instrumental in our success, both with colleagues and customers. This requires an enormous amount of time, effort, and maintenance.

Individuals who make up an organization are universally accepted as any institution's greatest asset, and yet, far too many employees are underutilized. Equally as bad is a workforce that is at such odds with one another that the organization's full potential may never be reached. Teamwork and delegation play important parts in providing quality leisure services in pleasant, low-stress work environments. Their proper implementation helps develop the individual, the team, and the business, ultimately ending in a win-win situation for all concerned.

Volunteers

The term volunteer incorporates a wide range of people: employees who work extra hours, student interns, sponsors, members who offer professional advice, people who provide services with no financial compensation, and so on. Volunteers play an integral role in many areas of the leisure profession by providing an economical plethora of labor and experience. With today's shrinking budgets and subsidies, the careful cultivation of a volunteer workforce continues to grow in importance. For many of us, planned projects or events could not be followed through without the work, knowledge, and time donated by volunteers.

Using the full potential of a volunteer workforce can expand your services, bring about closer ties with your community, increase your organization's opportunities, and provide an enormous amount of manpower. However, acquiring and using volunteers takes solid organization and planning. Not only is this necessary to begin the search for volunteers, it also is required so that no one's time is wasted throughout the task process. Nobody wants to waste their efforts in a confusing, unorganized operation; fewer things can ruin the search for volunteers like bad press or the rumor mill. Remember, volunteers give their time and talents by choice.

Proper planning facilitates essential information such as: who is needed, how many are needed, how long they will be needed, where they will be placed, what exactly is needed, and what is involved. Plan on taking a substantial amount of time to coordinate volunteer hours. The amount of liability must also be determined. All organizations that use volunteer labor are responsible not only for their volunteers' actions, but also any injuries suffered by these volunteers. Once the entire picture becomes more clear, action can be taken toward the recruitment of volunteers, the exact roles they will play, and the setup of any necessary protective measures.

Reprinted from the November 1996 issue of *Parks & Recreation* by special permission of the National Recreation and Park Association.

ACQUIRING VOLUNTEERS

Asking someone for help is often looked upon as a compliment. It is flattering to be told that your abilities are in demand. Most people do enjoy helping, particularly when they know that their labor and knowledge are genuinely needed and will be used effectively to do something of importance. The consideration of how you propose to retain a volunteer workforce might help in its acquisition. If the work required demands expertise in a certain area, begin your search at the places where this expertise can be found. A more general search can be utilized with broader strokes.

Advertising

Whether by word of mouth or through print, advertising is about the only way to convey the need for volunteers. Stick to the locations where you want to target your volunteer workforce in regard to age, education, sex, maturity, experience, etc.

- *Meetings* (employee meetings, committee meetings, community meetings, club meetings)
- *Notice boards* (at work, post offices, places of worship, community halls, markets, schools)
- *Newspapers/Magazines* (newsletters, trade journals, booklets, pamphlets, circulars)
- *Television/Radio* (Free airtime is given to plenty of worthwhile causes, particularly when a good story is involved. Unless you ask and provide a professional plan of what you are doing, it will not be!)
- *Corporate sponsors* (Publicity, and the interest it propagates, can be generated for all concerned parties when business gets involved. However, again, an organized plan must be presented.)
- *Posters* (Properly displayed notices in shops, walls, exits, even lavatories can be effective. ASK FIRST before you post.)

Community Groups

- *Religious groups* (Every church, mosque, or synagogue contains those who are seeking to fulfill a need for becoming involved in some type of community work.)

- *Boy Scouts/Girl Scouts* (Children may not have much experience, but there is plenty they can do.)
- *Clubs/Organizations* (Search the phone book for specific groups. Quite often they are looking for activities to become involved with or ways to help that utilize their areas of expertise.)
- *Schools/Colleges/Universities* (Contact lecturers, teachers, on-campus groups, etc., to help spread the word. Remind them that volunteering and subsequent experience gained will enhance any curriculum vitae.)

Individuals

- *Friends/Relatives/Employees* (But remember, you probably want to keep them as such.)
- *Parents/Children* (One usually involves the other.)
- *Ask around* (Seek out those who might be interested, including those individuals and groups who have taken part before.)

Do not forget to fully discuss why volunteers are needed and what is hoped to be accomplished. You may even be able to turn your request into their idea. Focus on the good things that will come about when the project is over. Ensure the work is necessary. Do not wear out your welcome and do not force the issue. Interview and select your volunteers carefully.

Just because they are "free" does not mean expenses will not occur. Treat the filling of volunteer positions as you would any job vacancy. Develop a good reputation for treating volunteers well. Throw them a party when everything has been completed. Why not offer prizes for the group and/or individual who donates the most work hours? Make it a friendly game or contest. Keep in mind that everyone must feel that he or she is a winner by having provided a valuable contribution. Let the community or volunteers know how they will benefit from *their* work and give full credit to all concerned.

KEEPING VOLUNTEERS

The sharing and distribution of information is the first step toward volunteer retention. A thorough orientation is a good idea. Make the orientation active and involving. Involvement demands that everyone has a good idea as to what is happening, why it is being done that way, and his or her role within the project. Almost all of us in the leisure industry have volunteered previously. Remember the time you became involved in helping out at a volunteer function? How did it feel to not be on top of things? Would you want to return to this situation? Neither do your volunteers. Let them know exactly what it is they are required to do through effective communication (e.g., listening and responding well to questions). Limit those in "authority" and avoid the constant bossing around of volunteers by paid employees. It is much easier to retain volunteers than it is to find them.

To further understand how to keep volunteers, it is vital to know why people want to volunteer. Since money is not often involved, there are any number of reasons why individuals will freely give their precious time. Ask them. Combating loneliness, utilizing the most of free time as a stepping stone to further self-interests, wanting to "spread the word," or just wishing to help are all valid reasons.

It is up to you to treat volunteers with respect and dignity, to politely discover the reasons why your organization was chosen, and to fulfill the needs of your volunteer workers. Satisfying these prerequisites will keep your volunteers coming back, often bringing recruits with them. This is what can separate your business from the myriad of others that search for free help. Recognition in satisfying volunteer needs is the key to both acquiring volunteers and keeping them. More often than not, people volunteer because they want to get involved and be accepted. Actively fulfill these and other needs.

Even the most resolute Samaritan likes to be thanked; most of us would like a bit more than that. Despite proclamations of embarrassment or "that is not necessary," volunteers do enjoy (or desire) tokens of appreciation. This involves the distribution of thank-you letters, certificates of appreciation, or the awarding of small plaques or gifts at an awards ceremony; it need not be expensive. My former department used to ask for and receive donations for "coupons" representing free meals, products, services, and discounts from a variety of local businesses. These were used as awards in contests and raffles and distributed at our volunteer award presentations. Even unclaimed lost-and-found items were used for this purpose (with care). Everyone involved received something. The least expensive recognition and one that is sometimes forgotten is the constant and sincere verbal acknowledgment of all the work that is being done by each individual. Acknowledging and rewarding individual accomplishments are powerful incentives in motivation and retention.

Volunteering is not always intrinsically driven. While attending university many years ago, I wanted to join a local health club but could not afford membership. I introduced myself to the owner and offered to work for him every Saturday in exchange for a membership. It took some persistence, but he eventually agreed.

Several months later, I asked him why his business was not open on Sundays. "I can't afford it," was the reply. The truth was he probably could not afford to be closed because most members had their Sundays free to enjoy and use the facilities. "You know," I said quietly, "there is a university in this town with over 20,000 students of which a sizable number are in need of local businesses where they can perform necessary internships." Within two months of concerted efforts, the health club opened seven days a week with expanded hours, thanks to the staggered schedules of new "volunteers" all needing to complete rigid scholastic requirements for graduation. Improvement suggestions by the volunteers greatly contributed to the club's success. Several of their friends joined the club as members. Both sides ended up happy; both sides got what they needed.

Twelve years later, I still have the thank-you card the club's owner gave me, something he never gave anyone else. I did not make a dime during the two years there, but the friendships made, the experience/confidence gained, and the sense of accomplishment I acquired are carried with me to this very day. It marked the first time that anyone had ever listened and followed through with one of my ideas, and it kept me volunteering long after I needed to be. Having ideas recognized and implemented was worth more than words can convey. Do this with your volunteers and they will come back.

TREATING VOLUNTEERS

Volunteers are not second-rate employees. They must be treated with kindness and gratitude because volunteers do not need you as much as you need them. Volunteers often have other commitments pertaining to jobs, families, and friends, and their time is a precious commodity. Use it well. Treat volunteers with understanding and flexibility. Do not angrily insist on their punctuality. Instead, let them want to be reliable by letting them know how important their work is and how much is dependent on it. (You should already be doing this with your regular, paid employees.) Do not be afraid to delegate responsibility. Responsibility and trust are highly motivational. Constantly standing over people's shoulders is annoying and displays a lack of trust and respect. Handle a volunteer as you would a customer.

Volunteers turn into customers. Those who already are customers can have their loyalty strengthened by becoming "part owners" through their work. When a volunteer becomes involved in a project, that involvement generates a level of interest in your business or organization which was previously unknown. This permeates throughout the volunteer's family and social circles, creating the potential to generate more business. The ability exists to create hundreds of "salesmen" who represent your concerns. I have been to several small festivals, fund-raisers, and clean-up drives where the only participants were those connected in one way or another to the volunteers. Nothing can make or break the reputation you have in your community like word of mouth.

By developing and using common sense guidelines and management practices, the majority of problems that are sometimes associated with volunteers will be eliminated. These include short-term commitments, high turnover resulting in constant retraining, added legal liabilities, jobs not well done, and too many people doing their own thing or reinventing the wheel. Trained and informed employees are not apt to fear for job security from volunteers looking for their generosity to be rewarded with employment. A properly managed group of volunteers provided with clear-cut goals, instructions, and training presents a veritable treasure for those planning projects, no matter how big or small. All it takes is a basic understanding of volunteers and volunteering and its processes. Once you have made the commitment to the whole picture involved in regard to selecting and working with volunteers, you are on the road to success. "Pay" volunteers with that which they seek, and you and your organization will be rewarded immeasurably. Volunteers can be the serendipitous outcome of a happy and organized workforce.

Finance and Accountants

Relax, this is not a lesson in finance and accounting principles. There are hundreds of books already available on that subject. This is an explanation of the importance of sound financial practices and how those who work with numbers often have to think. Because I am not an accountant, it may be a bit biased, but experience in having to work with and be responsible for the bottom line helped me to better understand the role of the finance department and its people. The integral part that responsible financing plays in any business also became more apparent.

Once realized, the usefulness of proper record keeping and the information these records contain can be used to benefit the entire organization. Few decisions should be made without a thorough investigation into the financial implications that all decisions will have on the business and its people. But, do you, your workers, and your finance people get along?

There is an old story that is told about a balloonist who became lost and landed in an empty field. The balloonist asked someone from the gathering crowd to tell him where he was. "You are in a balloon in the middle of an empty field," came a reply from a spectator. "You must be an accountant," said the balloonist, "for what you just told me is completely accurate, completely useless, and what I had already suspected." "And you," said the spectator, "must be a manager, because you have flown a balloon which you obviously had no control over and you now want me to help you with where you are going."

Differences in perspective, as this story demonstrates, are one explanation of why friction develops between individuals and departments. Those individuals who work in finance probably take most of the rap when someone is blamed for being "obstinate." There are many reasons for this, but perhaps the most common one is that most people do not understand the workings of finance and accounting and therefore fear appearing foolish when the subject arises (which it inevitably does). This need not be the case because accounting is little more than basic mathematics. Accounting is the international language of business and is a basic business tool. Every enterprise has to be able to maintain and present accurate records. There is no getting away from it. Every organization, whether it is profit or nonprofit, private or charitable, religious or governmental, requires an accountant.

Accountants keep track of all business transactions involving monetary assets by organizing, maintaining, recording, and analyzing financial activities. Monetary assets are comprised of the property, equipment, and goods owned by the business that have monetary value. Financial activities include all monetary transactions that enter or exit the company. This encompasses a wide variety of areas including: *payroll, tax preparation and payment, pensions, costs, inventory control, keeping track of sales, monthly financial statements (record keeping), cash flows, strategic planning, investments (preparing for growth), appraisals and assessments, the organization's banking, etc.*

Paying attention to the details of this information helps determine the efficiency of the business in four very important ways:

- It measures success.
- It helps point out any weaknesses.
- It can indicate areas that need improvement.
- It can help to anticipate crises.

How? A common theme throughout most companies in financial distress is, almost always, a lack of financial control and discipline. Paying attention to the details of this information can reveal:

- poor inventory control,
- theft,
- the need for the collection of money owed (a surprisingly large problem),
- the use of little or no planning (poor decision making), and
- inaccurate record keeping (resulting in outside audits/penalties among other things).

Accountants keep track of the details of this information. Problems that result from a lack of good record keeping can be discovered during the periodic rechecking of financial records—called an audit. During my tenure heading Recreation Services in Saudi Arabia, problems occasionally arose with a few of the supervisors at the different off-site areas concerning financial audits that were done on a routine basis. No amount of persuasion could sway the beliefs of some of these supervisors that audits were being done to ensure they were not stealing anything. Many times I had to accompany the accountant to the area where the audit was being done to keep the peace. It was a problem that was only partially solved. Nobody likes being audited. Yet audits have to be done regularly to check figures, review findings, make corrections, and every other reason mentioned. They should be regarded as being helpful and necessary, not as an inconvenience or an inquisition, and serendipity can always apply.

During one audit, I happened to mention to the performing accountant that the business was having a great deal of trouble organizing an overseas shipment. The manufacturer stated that equipment could not be shipped without payment, and company policy dictated that payment could not be made until shipment was received. The accountant, using his knowledge and skills with banking procedures, set up a letter of credit using a neutral bank as an intermediary to hold and release the payment. The equipment was shipped without any problems.

In all businesses, useful information regarding the amount of money that is collected, spent, or stored in various areas and ways is presented on a *balance sheet,* suggesting that the amount of money coming in should balance with what is going out (or else). It is the responsibility of every employee to learn how to read financial records (balance sheets). They are not a difficult thing to learn. Common sense dictates that balance sheets should be very straightforward.

A friend of mine once relayed the story about a vice president of finance who worked for a large company. This vice president did not have "people skills" and she was not well liked by many people in the company. In order to maintain job security, she developed an accounting system that was so complicated it could be used to confuse and belittle anyone who questioned its setup. This accounting system did work, as did her underhanded scheme to stay with the company—at least for awhile. She was a very bright woman, and no one could accuse her otherwise, but eventually the unnecessary complexity of the system led to her dismissal when her superiors finally had enough. Today's news reports tell of other good examples. For instance, some modern-day film companies make movies that generate hundreds of millions of dollars, only to have creative accountants claim that there were no profits. Cases such as these help develop the friction between the finance department and those who work outside of it.

Financial information does concern everyone within the organization and should be considered as part of the process of employee involvement. Numerous case studies exist that detail the outright shock from employees who, after being shown their employer's balance sheets, come to the previously unimaginable realization that most of the money the business collects goes straight back into the business via expenses and growth, not into the back pockets of a few executives. Other benefits from this realization are established as well. When everybody knows and understands the financial numbers, there is less room for underhandedness (including theft) and a greater appreciation of costs and expenses.

Perhaps the most controversial aspect of accountants and accounting is the way that working with numbers requires one to think. Because the discipline almost exclusively involves the flow and control of money (in one form or another) and its balance, there is a tendency for the finance folks to only see the financial side of things. (It is human nature to sometimes only see one side of things.) It can therefore be occasionally difficult to convince an accountant of the money that could be generated by a good idea.

To an accountant, ideas are not something substantial with a monetary value that can be recorded in a ledger book. As an example of this, a major international hotel chain once ran into difficulties between its hotel managers and its finance and accounting people. The hotel managers wanted a costly renovation project to be financed that would revitalize numerous meeting and banquet areas at each of their operations. This had been a proven revenue-producing area of the market and it was growing by leaps and bounds. Unfortunately, because many of the different hotel's meeting and banquet rooms were in such poor state, these same hotels could not generate market share due to competition from other hotels and businesses.

No amount of discussion could convince the accountants that the costly renovations were needed. According to the "figures" and "estimates," the accountants said, these renovations would prove to be a money loser. Eventually, after much consultation between both parties, the chairman decided to go ahead with the projects. They turned out to be a great success by generating an increase in revenues greater than the construction costs.

Perhaps one of the most difficult aspects of explaining the turnarounds I have led is in presenting the importance of the bottom line. My methods often contradict this. Usually, I just want to know if an area is making or losing money. I then set out to correct the problem, if money is being lost, by focusing on the situation that leads to money loss, not on the fact that money must be made or saved. *There are too many managers who chase after money thinking that customers and/or solutions will follow when, in fact, it is actually the other way around.* In other words—solve the cause, not its outcome.

Business books are full of studies depicting beleaguered companies that failed because too much emphasis was placed on the bottom line. "Numbers" became not only an end, but the means to an end. When this happens, the implementation of new ideas and the risk that often accompanies it is never realized. Stagnation results. Organizations cannot grow without taking risks, and that involves taking financial risks. It is not the duty of accountants to take into consideration the "spirit," "determination," "gut feelings," or "personal insight" that drives organizations, nor should we ask them to. The critical role of the accountant is to gather, study, and maintain accurate financial information so that this information can be used accordingly.

The moral of the story, as with much of this book, is that a balance between employees and their specializations is vitally important for organizational and business success. A firm commitment should be made to incorporate many different employee and department's opinions, factors, and considerations. This is true particularly when it comes to finances because throughout all areas of the organization, it is essential that an eye always be kept on the money which is raised and used to operate that organization. Otherwise, the business may well find itself out of business. Business (and our jobs) cannot survive without proper finance and accounting.

The Importance of Marketing

Despite all that may be said and heard, good products or services do not sell themselves. We have all probably witnessed this in action before: a wonderful program, activity, product, or service is conceived only to wither and die after development. No matter how good an idea is, unless proper marketing principles are utilized, success can prove to be an elusive goal.

Marketing is a complex process and, as with leisure, its breadth makes it difficult to define. In a business sense, marketing concentrates on the marketplace and is partially comprised of selling and advertising. Its purpose is to bring a seller and a buyer together. These needs are then interpreted so that those responsible for producing a product or service create a desired, and hopefully profitable, result. In other words, it is smarter for the business to offer what customers want, not what the business wants to sell.

Marketing provides the framework that is used to represent the product/service and the organization which offers that product/service through some form of advertisement. The process that helps organize and plan this outcome is commonly known as the marketing mix. Sectioned into four basic elements, this mix is referred to as the four P's, and they require much customer involvement. (Because of the uniqueness of the leisure industry and its businesses, another three P's are added for our use.) Customer Involvement means more than questionnaires and suggestion boxes, which often do little more than gather the odd complaint. (Effective questionnaires demand expert planning and complete follow-through.) You must actively pursue customer interaction to maximize the possible benefits resulting from the use of the four P's:

- Product • Place • Price • Promotion
- People • Physical Environment • Process

PRODUCT (OR SERVICE)

Know the product/service and its desired outcome: Is the desired outcome education based? Is it geared toward competition? Having fun? Creating something? Meeting people? The same product/service can appeal to those with differing benefit perceptions. Are you aware of them? Are you targeting families? Single persons? Different age groups (children, teens, senior citizens)? What is your target group's lifestyle? Its income level? Is the product/service of high quality? Does it meet customers' desired needs and wants?

PLACE
(THE LOCATION OR DISTRIBUTION OF THE PRODUCT/SERVICE)

The location should be convenient to the clientele. It should contain everything needed for the program. The activity should be presented at an appropriate time and not conflict with holidays, festivals, or major sporting events. A backup location is also a good idea (or a rain-check date and time). (See "Physical Environment.")

PRICE
(OR PERCEIVED VALUE)

Prices are never set in stone and reflect the degree of benefit as seen by customers. Other considerations include the financial income of your target group. Do you wish to be exclusive? Competitive? Discount? If you are nonprofit or complimentary, will the value of what you are offering change the behavior of prospective participants enough to facilitate involvement?

PROMOTION
(ADVERTISING, PUBLICITY, SELLING)

With promotion, the effective use of communication is essential in producing results. Good advertising creates awareness and an incentive for the consumer to take action. Will your advertising be done through word of mouth? Posters? Announcements? Printed advertisements in journals, magazines, or newspapers? Radio? Television? How about "spreading the word" through group discounts, corporate memberships, competitions, prizes, giveaways, two-for-ones, etc.? Who will you use to sell the product/service? Members, staff, professional marketers? Advertising is done throughout the organization, and everyone and everything can and should be used. Regardless of its form, advertising requires constant maintenance and adjustment.

PEOPLE
(CUSTOMER-SERVICE STAFF WHO ARE PART OF THE PRODUCT/SERVICE)

All staff members should be neat and presentable. Clean and pressed uniforms or some type of shirt, hat, or other garment that designates an individual as a staff member is a good idea. Staff members should always be friendly and courteous and be sincere with their warmth and positive attitude. They should be the type of people who enjoy helping others as well as being a part of a team.

PHYSICAL ENVIRONMENT
(PHYSICAL SURROUNDINGS AND AMBIANCE OF WHERE THE PRODUCT/SERVICE IS OFFERED)

How customers view your facilities is a powerful marketing force. Rooms, meeting areas, and the facilities themselves should be clean, hygienic, safe, and tidy. Equipment should be safe and in good working order. Walls should be free of too many posters and signs. The air should be fresh and clean smelling (no kidding). Even things as trivial as ensuring that paper towels and toilet paper are always in the disposal units is important. Customers will probably not notice these things if they are consistently provided for them, but if they are not, their absence will produce a negative image of you and your business.

PROCESS
(OPERATIONAL MATTERS AFFECTING
CUSTOMER PERCEPTIONS)

Staff friendliness, appointment and cancellation systems, customer waiting times, etc., all fall under this category. These are the types of in-house marketing systems that can make or break a leisure business. I have heard that studies have been done which report that a business can possibly lose one-fifth of its customers if its products are of cheap or shoddy manufacture, but two-thirds of customers will be lost if the service itself is perceived as being bad.

Throughout the marketing process, every step must be directed toward targeting and satisfying customers. Knowing what the customer wants helps identify opportunities. These opportunities are researched to uncover any strengths and weaknesses; the results are then matched with the business's abilities. The result is then *targeted,* through advertising, to a segment of the market where success is envisioned. (Scattershot approaches can be very ineffective.) This is accomplished through what is called benefit segmentation.

In essence, the benefits perceived by the potential customer are used to sell the service/product. Fast-food restaurants provide good examples. Carefully watch the television commercials that advertise the products of these businesses. Many are actually promoting, or trying to sell, a low price or a dining experience (especially when they are targeting children) or convenience. Few actually comment on the taste of the food.

The longevity of products/services also figures prominently. Marketing recognizes that most products/services are not eternal and often suffer through a birth, midlife, and death. Prolonging this trend relies on a marketing technique known as the three U's (business theoreticians love these letter gimmicks), all of which involve the previously mentioned "four P's" customer process (here demonstrated by example):

• Uses • Users • Usage

Uses

Basic children's programs and equipment requiring teamwork and cooperation can, with a few minor adjustments, become ready-made adult activities targeted toward managers paying to focus on activities demanding leadership, group interaction, and team effort. The *uses* of the equipment and program are then increased.

Users

Remember when exercise was something only athletes or those on the fringe of society pursued? Now exercise programs are targeted at those interested in weight reduction, illness recovery, health and longevity, dating, stress reduction, and other benefit perceptions developed to increase the number of *users* of exercise-oriented services and products.

Usage

Swimming pools and large rooms often sit vacant during set periods of time. Add decorations, change the lighting, throw a party/dinner/get-together, or contract out to local craftsmen or vendors and these areas are then the perfect vehicles for other revenue or guest activity enhancements. Various forms of *usage* have been adapted and made profitable. This diversity can help to provide a new image for your business.

Image is probably the first aspect of marketing and the most powerful one your customer will initially encounter. What kind of reputation do you have? Is your advertising truthful and does it accurately represent your offerings? Do you honor your words and/or claims? Are the interior and exterior of your premises clean and tidy? What impression is made upon entering the front door? Are the walls of your business covered with signs or are they smart and professional looking? Do your employees present a professional look and attitude and are they helpful and attentive? These are the types of free advertising that generate additional revenues from friends and associates of current customers.

Looking at your competitors is highly beneficial and is yet another area that interests marketers. Why not research the competition? Knowing how other similar businesses have succeeded or failed and why they have can save a lot of time and expense. In fact, almost everything within and outside of a business could play a part in effective marketing if the correct application is used.

Good marketing is of great importance in the leisure industry and is a highly effective tool when its implications and purpose are fully understood and used. Everyone who is convinced of the importance of marketing and encouraged and directed toward the same goals and objectives should take part. The more people that are involved, the easier it is to appreciate the wants and needs of prospective customers and to create the ideas and methods that will satisfy them, as well as to inform them that the product/service exists.

The last stage, and arguably the most important, is the sale (or sometimes in leisure's case, participation). A sale marks the final act of acceptance. This is what business thrives on. How you choose to make the sale is a personal call. Some organizations like to use pressure; some let the customer decide. Either way, the completion of the sale (hopefully in an ethical manner) provides the money that finances business operations (particularly wages). What happens afterward is equally crucial. It is easier to retain customers than it is to create them, and an emphasis always needs to be directed toward customer retention ("custom" also has a birth, midlife, and death). Marketing concerns itself with these significant matters. Marketing is a fascinating and lengthy subject, and although we have only scratched the surface here, the acceptance of its value to the organization is an important step toward piecing together and understanding the successful business as a whole. By becoming fully acquainted with your organization's products and services and the needs of your customers, marketing creates and develops a vast array of possibilities and successes that may, as yet, lie unseen.

RETAINING AND EXPANDING
CURRENT CUSTOMER INTEREST

Although it is normal human nature to enjoy the comfortable repetitiveness of the familiar, sooner or later the desire will come, for most people, to look to other horizons and try something new. This is particularly true with customers, whose needs and wants can be ever changing.

Retaining customers is a valuable aspect of every business. It is far easier to retain a customer than it is to create one, with most estimations claiming that it costs five times as much to gain a new customer than it does to retain a current one. Retention, therefore, is an important aspect of the marketing campaign. Target marketing your current customers may appear odd at first, but continuously providing "marketing maintenance" to those who willingly pay for your services on a regular basis helps ensure that they will continue to do so. Regular customers are relatively easy to communicate with and approach, and they are an important source of feedback in providing the information as to whether or not your programs are on the right track.

Customer Retention and Marketing

Benefit perception emphasis is the basis of all advertising. Marketers know that customers perceive products and services in terms of benefits (benefit perception). Customers weigh in their minds the benefits they believe they can obtain from your service and act accordingly. If the benefit matches their wants or needs, they will usually purchase what is offered. Learn to read the benefits sought by your customers and change your programs and advertising accordingly. Customers may not be aware of additional benefits that arise from your services. For example, the game of golf could be itemized and adapted into specified programs that spotlight different benefits as follows:

- Recreational: Members simply wish to get away from it all and enjoy a favorite pastime.
- Competitiveness: Some members may only appreciate the competitive nature of the game.
- Socializing: Particularly in a group-play situation (perhaps adjusted to age, gender, new neighbors, employees), golf—as are most recreation activities—is an excellent way to develop social contacts.
- Business Relations: Golf is often used for "social business work," and members can conduct business in an informal, relaxed setting.
- Career Student: Some members will enjoy taking lessons, but do not actually play much golf.
- Follow the Group: Members participate not because they are interested in golf, but because other people are.

• Something New: Members who joined the Club for one activity (swimming), may become interested in another (golf).

Customer involvement. It is difficult for most people to give up what they are involved with, and the same applies with customers. If customers are truly involved with your programs, their feelings of "ownership" in those programs is a powerful retention device. Customers become involved and feel ownership in your business:

• when their needs are met;
• when they are listened to;
• when they are greeted and treated as friends;
• when their comments, complaints, or suggestions are taken seriously (acted upon);
• when they are asked for their input; and
• when they are made to feel unique.

Committees. In several types of recreational settings it is normal (and sometimes expected) for participants to be asked to serve on committees or boards whose purpose is to assist with the direction of the business or in the alleviation of the problems of major undertakings. This is another form of "ownership" that makes the volunteer participant feel that he or she is an integral part of the operation.

Sales competitions. The use of marketing competitions that offer prizes, free memberships, or other incentives to members who achieve sales objectives required by the business will often get current members involved in advertising. This type of retention device uses current customers to actively promote the business and is usually seen in the form of offering compensation for every new member who signs on or to the current member who brings in the most new members during a set period of time (a contest). People are often proud of their leisure associations and interests and will try to get others interested in them as well. Tapping into this human desire acts as both a customer retention tool and a way to bring in new customers.

Promotions. Offering members special discounts and other "financial deals" is a good incentive to get them to try new things or continue with the old ones. Just because a customer is already a customer does not mean that the types of regular marketing necessities and gimmicks used to promote your business do not still apply. Don't be afraid to try and use different aspects of your full marketing arsenal in maintaining customer retention.

Volunteers can be instrumental in leisure business. Sometimes an event or program cannot go on without them. When I was the director of a large equestrian operation some time ago, we had several of our former members become volunteer instructors. They were offered free memberships and a percentage of the revenues they helped bring in as compensation. Far from losing out on each of these volunteers' annual membership fees, the Ranch benefited enormously from these "inexpensive employees," who actually created more business for us. Each acted as a separate salesperson, bringing in family members, friends, and associates who originally had not joined. This enabled us to expand our current programs. Again, the feeling of "ownership" in the business was a pivotal force for these volunteers.

Change. Adapting and changing recreation programs can eliminate the tedium and boredom that may develop from constant, regular participation. Almost everyone likes to be formally challenged, and doing so can revitalize current customers and the employees who work with them. Perhaps a new time to offer the program is appropriate, or a new location. Focusing on a different aspect of the program than usual may spark renewed interest, as may bringing in different activity leaders. Offering incremental programs set up in certain stages, where the participant "graduates" to a higher level after a period of time, is not only an incentive for desiring change on the customer's part, but also expands your program. Whatever is decided, it is of the utmost importance that you are in direct contact with your participants and fully understand their wishes. Change is almost always resisted when it is not understood or appreciated, and you could end up losing your customers.

Specialized Courses—"The Ten-Session Course Plan"

There are a myriad of plans and strategies that can be stored in the leisure business arsenal to retain customers. Your employees probably have many creative ideas. Using everything at the business's disposal at one time is not practical. It is best to try each strategy as thoroughly as possible before moving on to another one, and it is always necessary to have another plan, variation, or strategy. Do you have a plan for developing and/or retaining customer interest and participation once they begin to fade?

When the novelty of activities or programs beings to wear thin, customer participation often declines as a result. This can happen no matter how wonderful the activity and translates into a loss of revenue for the business. Customers have other priorities and commitments and are constantly bombarded with offers to spend their time and money elsewhere. If they are somewhere else, your business loses its revenue.

One way to help maintain customer interest (and revenues) is through "ten-session" courses. A ten-session course is designed as a complete service package. It does not have to run ten sessions; it can be of any duration. *The point is to lock in the customer* using value and prices, over a set period of time, with a specific goal or purpose in mind. You may even choose to use a coupon-type booklet to achieve the same effect. Courses have virtually no limitations and can be designed for golf, tennis, fitness, and almost any other recreation program. Always, they must be adjusted to the needs, skill level, age, maturity, and intensity of the participants.

The goal or purpose of the course is the selling point or benefit perceived by the customer. For example, offering a ten-week course in learning equestrian jumping explains the purpose of the course. Writing down and presenting the particulars of the course as well as an obtainable goal helps clarify the course's intentions even further. Courses could start with the basics of jumping including flat-work, position, learning about the types of jumps, and then working on the jumping itself, with the objective of jumping an obstacle of one meter as the final goal. Or the course could be designed around fine-tuning and improving jumping techniques for the serious competitor who wishes to perform better in tournaments. *Staying in touch with your customer base ensures that the course is designed around what your customers actually want.*

Courses are of benefit to the business because once payment is made the revenue has been received whether the customer participates or not (be careful to always encourage participation). Courses allow groups of similar-minded customers to pursue their own interests and not follow the direction of larger groups. Courses add variety and a "specialness" to set programs and activities for both the customer and the instructing employee. Everyone likes to be formally challenged from time to time, and properly planned and organized courses can fit the bill. Courses should end with the awarding of certificates and perhaps a fun-oriented competition or social function as well.

It is probably best to use courses as a second resort to enhance and improve regularly scheduled activities and programs. Courses are better used as a retention tool, not as a membership selling point (although this rule is not set in stone). Although the outsider can certainly be persuaded to participate in a course, and that persuasion *can* lead to an interest in membership, without a knowledge of what your potential customers want, it is difficult to design an appropriate course. Designing a course without knowing your customers' wishes more often than not results in offering a course geared toward the instructor, with the resulting difficulties in finding paying participants.

Experiment with course design by finding out what your customers want. Use your present activities and programs as a guide to what they need. Used properly, interesting, informative, and motivational courses can enhance and expand any leisure business program.

Whatever direction is chosen in maintaining customer retention, remember to keep retention as one of your top priorities. It can be easy to lose sight of current, valuable customers while searching for new customers. Customers are the most important part of every business. Without them, there is no business. By learning to retain your current customer base, you will be on the right track in retaining your business's solvency.

Pricing and How to Make It Work Best for You

For some people in the leisure industry, pricing strategy involves little more than a gut feeling. Perhaps the cost of providing the services and what any competitors charge might be taken into consideration. This type of approach is unfortunate because few decisions affect immediate consumer acceptance or rejection of your program than prices.

Often the very success of the leisure business depends upon the perceptions customers have as to how much the service or program will cost. Despite this, few leisure teams give pricing very much thought, and even then, the same old approach that has been used for years is usually implemented. With a little effort, however, it is possible to make pricing work for your leisure business in a variety of ways.

Before the pricing process begins, it is necessary to stop and consider exactly what you want pricing to do for your business. The obvious answer is to increase income. But, how will this be done? By improving sales? By being more competitive? By attracting and targeting a specific clientele? By getting more customers to try your programs and services? By developing and maintaining a proper image? By actually lowering demand? (Offering too much could be a detraction.) How about a combination of one or more of these objectives? If you are serious enough to make the most of the prices you will use, then it is worth the time and effort to consider these questions and to write them down and discuss them with your colleagues. By doing this, you not only get valuable input from fellow employees (and greater commitment on their part), you will also have a written guide that can be used to measure whether your pricing decisions are compatible with your objectives.

At the beautiful Trio Ranch Country Club, located in Jeddah, Saudi Arabia, the owners wanted to increase membership while at the same time maintain some exclusivity. Although two of the programs (equestrian sports and golf) were not readily available elsewhere for most prospective customers in the vicinity, these potential members did have access to other recreation facilities in the area. Apparently what they did not have, they did not miss, and it was difficult to attract their attention toward the ranch. What the owners needed convincing of was that they could not afford to let their prices determine member selection. A balance needed to be established, which was reflected in their prices, between the high standards offered (a proper image) and customer attraction.

The ranch was about a twenty-five minute drive from Jeddah's city center; most customers thought this was too far. Although much revenue was generated from national and local competitions and tournaments, the ranch's owners wanted a stronger membership base. In effect, they needed a pricing strategy. When I was called in, we involved virtually every aspect of the business in establishing this strategy: finance, sales, employees, and customers. Effective pricing decisions involve all of these areas. Cooperation, work ownership, and teamwork are always essential. Here is what we considered in establishing new prices:

COSTS

Costs are the base component of prices. Prices cannot be effectively determined without a full understanding of your cost structure. This means equipment and material costs, wear and tear (depreciation), labor, utilities, etc. Even the costs of marketing and other costs "outside" the direct path of the creation and running of the program/service need to be factored in. Cost structures for each program should be analyzed. Do not rely on across-the-board averages. Variations can and do exist from program to program, no matter how similar they are.

CUSTOMERS AND GUESTS

Without customers there would be no businesses, no jobs, and no paychecks, no matter how wonderful the service. Customers are the ultimate judge in determining if your prices reflect good value, and they will act accordingly. Do not be afraid to simply ask your customers for their input. This can be done professionally and discreetly without the use of the often misused "answer to everything" questionnaire. Try to determine customers' high and low perceptions of an acceptable price. Factor in the other considerations that customers use in decision making. What will it cost them in terms of time and travel to get to your business? Is it prudent to comparison shop? Will they have to make payments? How much will it cost them to switch from their old product/service to yours? Will there be any additional (or hidden) costs? These questions will be considered by most customers. Learn to think like your clientele; then recognize any opportunities or challenges.

COMPETITORS

Know and appreciate what your potential customers see as an alternative or replacement. Few things can make or break your business as competition can. Remember that it is not unheard of for some businesses to actually have to lower prices below cost for a period of time just to stave off the competition. And there is *always* competition. One fatal mistake sometimes made by managers or owners in the leisure industry is to be so proud and enamored of their own business and programs that they think customers will be lining up at the front door. This NEVER happens. But proper pricing can help pique the customers' interest and help get them to your door. Competition has other interpretations as well; it may not mean that there is another company or program trying to gain your market share. It might involve competing against any attitudes your customers have. They may have their own way of viewing money and value and never see your way of thinking (or pricing). Again, try to understand how and what *they* think is a fair price.

COMPATIBILITY

A final step to pricing is to stand back and ensure that all aspects of what was used to determine the price work together. Go back to your original written objectives. Are your prices compatible with them? Have all areas of financing, marketing, sales, etc., been consulted and considered? What about the people who actually administer the program and deal one on one with your customers? Have they been consulted? Check and be sure.

Think you are ready to begin setting prices? Think again. There are a myriad of ways that prices are used. It is in your best interest to consider all of them. Look at how other programs and services use pricing and think about how you can adopt them. Always be on the lookout for new strategies and objectives. Let your prices work for you. In business school, so many types of pricing are discussed that it defies memorization. Here are what some of my notes, adjusted for the leisure industry, look like. Think about and discuss how they might benefit the different areas of your programs:

Type of Pricing	Definition	Explanation/Examples
Breakdown	Prices are broken down into palatable segments.	A $1,000 membership is sold in installments (4 payments of $250) or explained as costing less than $2.75 a day.
Seasonal	Price adjusted during certain time periods.	Prices rise during peak periods (seasons). Prices reduce during slow times (to encourage sales).
Pay One Price or Pay as You Go	Pay one price, get unlimited use.	Amusement parks are a good example. Either pay one fee at the gate and ride all the rides, or pay for each ride separately.
Bundling (Unbundling)	Sell services as a package deal or break up and sell separately.	Selling activities in designated lots such as ten aerobics lessons or five horseback riding lessons. Unbundling would be selling these activities as single units.

Exclusivity (Snob Appeal)	Customers pay for "exclusivity."	Premium prices for trendiness or what some people consider reflects high social esteem.
Discount	Low prices.	Customers buy because the price is low. Perhaps there is little value seen. They have low incomes or simply do not wish to spend much.
Captive	"Locking" in customers by initially selling cheap then charging a premium for necessary components.	Customer signs membership contract, then hidden costs are exposed. The classic example: Razor blade/shaving companies that sell the handles cheaply, but the blades that fit them are very expensive.
Psychological	Prices do not approach what is perceived as too much. Usually a number divisible by ten or some other taboo limit.	Charging $99 instead of $100. Listing members' prices next to what non-members pay.
Promotional	Not paying a set price.	Having constant sales, always bettering competitors' prices.
Value Added	Adding "freebies" or other incentives.	Two-for-one deals, allowing members special privileges, a "baker's dozen."
Trials	Ease the risk perceived by the customer to encourage participation and eventually a greater sale.	Two-month aerobic memberships. First tennis lesson free. First horse riding lesson at a discount.

Hidden Costs	Not displaying extra costs needed to complete the service.	Tips or taxes, charging additionally for previously unmentioned parts, labor, or necessary equipment.
Fixed to Variable	One set price begins the process; the next costs are determined by use.	Entrance fees followed by usage fees (e.g., pay to get into the disco, then for each drink).
Differential	Charge certain customers differently.	Members pay one price; nonmembers pay another.
Creative Variable	Setting prices according to a certain time or length in an imaginative way.	Decreasing the price according to the customers' stamina (e.g., selling submarine sandwiches by the inch; selling boaters marina space by the meter).
Price Performance	Price determined by value perception.	Museums or exhibits asking guests to use their discretion in offering a donation upon leaving.
Differing Segments	Same program sold differently (with different prices to differing customers).	Athletic lessons (tennis, aerobic, horse riding, etc.) priced for groups, children, adults, and senior citizens.
Product Line	Prices arranged to get customers to focus on the "deal."	Expensive goods or services are displayed next to more reasonably priced goods or services.

It should go without saying that only you and your leisure business can determine what pricing system can work best to attract the customers you want. Keep in mind that common sense and ethical behavior play key roles in how your customers will perceive your pricing strategy. Finally, do not sell yourself short. Think about how high you can reasonably go with prices rather than how low. Case studies do exist that show customers are actually turned away from making a purchase because they thought the price was too low and that something was wrong with the product. Establishing good customer relations is the start to understanding how these individuals think. Discuss and learn how this information can best help you. Never stop reanalyzing why and how your business came up with its prices, and do not be afraid to try new ways to achieve pricing satisfaction.

Ethics and Quality

Make a mental list of the people you know outside of your own family whom you admire. Think about what it is that sets them apart from others. Perhaps you admire their integrity or the fact that they can be counted on to be honest, fair, and dependable. Chances are that the people on your list are friends, those individuals with whom you have the choice to associate. Now take friendship out of the equation. How long would your list be of only those you have worked with were allowed on it? How many people in your current place of work do you respect or admire?

The term "friend" is bantered about in many workplaces as if it were the only glue that held organizations together. Realistically, however, most "friendships" within organizations tend to evaporate once the workday, or employment, ends. Yes, true friendships can and do develop among colleagues, but this is not what comprises the foundation for human interactions and relationships existing in the workplace. No organization can endure without some sense of integrity, respect, and a sense of morality among its employees. These are the traits that allow individuals to work cooperatively and willingly together toward a common purpose. And these traits comprise the meaning of ethics. Without ethics no business can expect to last for long. However, looking around the business arena today sometimes gives one the opposite impression.

By listening to the television or browsing through a newspaper, one cannot help but get the impression that the world appears to be lacking in ethics. The news is full of individuals or businesses that appear to have "made it" due to "alleged" illegalities or unethical behavior. Stories abound concerning companies that try to make more money by jeopardizing, in one way or another, the safety or well-being of human beings.

But this kind of behavior has a tendency to catch up with those who instigate it. These organizations or people are usually in the news because they have been caught and must now answer to their unethical personal conduct. With some people there is such a strong desire to "win" at any cost that any possible negative outcomes are considered worth the risk. Money becomes the overriding goal and objective. The results inevitably spread across the entire organization, and the finger of blame is soon pointing at anyone who either is or could be considered guilty. In essence, what went around came around. An old adage states that "nice guys finish last." This suggests that some type of underhandedness or immor ality must exist so that success can be obtained. Without any doubt, this could not be further from the truth. Almost always, it is the trusted ones who rise to a level of success and stay there.

Because customers are now better informed than ever before about the operations and practices of companies and businesses, and have more choice regarding where to take their business, the need to behave ethically only grows in importance. Ethics is being truthful, sincere, and unselfish. It consists of thinking of others, saying what is meant, and meaning what is said, and it simply must envelop everyone within an organization. How our behavior and the reputation of our business is perceived often decides if we can hold our heads up high among colleagues, friends, and family. This is a fundamental aspect of ethics, and it is both a personal and a group issue.

The question of how business is to be conducted is one that every organization faces. Ethics (or the lack of them) figure prominently in decision making. A good reputation is a precious thing to have. It is acquired by being earned. Honesty and integrity also have a direct effect on people involved with the business, both internally (employees) and externally (customers, contractors, suppliers). In decision making there are several questions any business is obliged to ask regarding the following areas:

- *Legality.* Is what you wish to do legal?
- *Fairness.* How will the decision's outcome affect the different people who are involved with it (employees, customers, the community, etc.)?
- *Self-Respect.* Do you feel good about the decision and its outcome? Are you proud of it?

- *Long-Term Effects.* Shortsighted solutions are rarely an answer. Will they create or destroy job security? Will they be dangerous or too risky? How is the environment affected?

Developing an ethical stance involves more than addressing a checklist. In addition, it involves a full explanation to employees as to what is and will be expected. One indisputable aspect regarding the practice of professionalism and ethics is its all-embracing single mindedness. Behaving professionally and acting ethically is an all-or-nothing campaign. Ethics cannot be acted upon part of the time. Yet ethics, and the professionalism that goes along with them, are not difficult to grasp or implement. Sometimes treating others in the manner in which you, yourself, would like to be treated is a first step. Questioning behavior and then acting to improve on it goes even further. By utilizing basic principles developed to help shape ethical behavior, the analysis and implementation of ethical solutions and actions is more readily understood:

- *Purpose.* The understanding and acceptance of the real reasons, objectives, or intentions for what is being done.
- *Empathy/Understanding.* Putting the feelings, consideration, and well-being of others into practice. Fully appreciating the outcomes of any actions or behaviors, and the effects these have on others.
- *Responsibility/Pride.* The sense of satisfaction and ownership that comes from a job well done. Maintaining self-esteem and wanting to be held accountable.
- *Commitment.* Not giving up. Remaining flexible to others' viewpoints, yet persistent with faith and beliefs.
- *Perspective.* The capacity to comprehend the whole picture and see what is really important. Understanding the need for cooperating with others both internally and externally.

Once the practice of behaving ethically has been established, new possibilities begin to unfold that can provide countless opportunities. (Would you not rather do business with an organization that is considered safe and reliable?)

Perhaps the greatest of these opportunities is the establishment of an organization that delivers total quality. Quality is defined as the achievement of excellence or distinguishing attributes. Is this not what we seek and strive for in our products and services as leisure professionals? Would it not be wonderful to reach and maintain such a high degree of ethics and professionalism that your organization is able to do most things right the first time by trusting fellow employees and without having to recheck everyone's work? These are the concepts of total quality.

The father of total quality is considered to be W. Edwards Deming. During World War II, Deming established spectacular results in various lines of production by believing in the value of employees. He stated that most troubles begin at the top by management who put more of an emphasis on numbers than they did on people. He proposed that superficial gimmicks and slogans often substituted for real improvements, ethical behavior, and teamwork, and that the common workplace, riddled with fear and shortsightedness, resisted innovation and change through counterproductive internal competition.

Deming put his talents to the test and found that employee respect, input, and involvement unleashed the kind of professionalism, flexibility, and improvements that could meet the challenges of competition and a changing marketplace head on. Unfortunately, when the war ended and the troops came home, the age-old practices of dictating from the top resumed. Deming continued to spread the word, yet few wanted to hear it.

Meanwhile, Japan was beginning its post-war recovery. Before the war, Japan had a terrible worldwide reputation for making cheap, shoddy goods. In fact, buying Japanese was the brunt of many jokes. With few resources and having to start almost literally from scratch, the Japanese decided to rebuild in a different way— one that would not merely replace what had already existed, but that would be better than before. Deming and his theories were called in. Most of Mr. Deming's life was spent working with the Japanese, and a discussion on this tiny country's current reputation for quality and productivity need not be made. Virtually everyone around the world is familiar with it. Most of this is due to the work of Mr. Deming. Today, the highest honor Japan can bestow upon a member of its business community is the W. Edwards Deming award for excellence.

The improvement of quality is an objective in every transformational situation. Transformational change cannot, and will not, take place in an environment lacking in ethics. Ethics and quality go hand in hand. Individuals or organizations simply cannot carry on without regard for fellow employees, customers, communities, and the earth. If the choice is made to do so, it is at their own peril. We all, as leisure professionals, need to care about our behavior, our actions, and the effects these have on the products and services we provide. What we do does eventually come back to us. Thinking through what we plan to do with the concerns of others in mind is a start to living and working professionally with little fear of embarrassment, humiliation, or destruction. Ethics help set the stage for successful transformation. After all, how many chances are there? Make ethics a central issue in your life and work.

Planning Projects, Events, and Activities

Initiating transformational change involves learning to do new things and to do many familiar things in different ways. Whether introducing changes in business operations or preparing and presenting established programs and activities differently, the task can prove to be a bit frightening. Often the best way to combat fear and insecurity in these situations is to break down the work into manageable steps. Planning a new or different project, event, or activity can be compared to preparing a meal. Whether this "meal" is envisioned as a complex gourmet feast or simple down-home fare, much of the difficulty lies in having all the different components come together at a planned time. The more people who are planning to eat, the more difficult the task. And once the meal gets going (or right beforehand), anything can and usually does happen.

Developing activities or events can be a complex process, especially if you are not experienced at that activity. However, it is not necessary to know everything there is to know about your planned activity. When preparing a meal, you do not need to know the process for manufacturing pepper, the best procedures for growing vegetables, or how to fashion silverware. What is required is the ability to manage and organize the expertise of those who do (whether this be employees, outside contractors, or advice from experts) and the capacity and determination to put them all together. In our example, choosing a recipe and planning a shopping trip pretty much takes care of preliminaries. In all program start-ups, proper planning is essential, so that it is not discovered that spoons are needed after the soup has been served.

The leisure or recreation sections of most libraries contain a wealth of information designed to help the leisure professional with creative program ideas designed for clientele of all ages and needs. Many professional organizations have lists available to the public that display the titles of numerous books and sources also containing enormously helpful information.

With so much available on this subject, it would be foolish to repeat here what is already discussed elsewhere. Instead we will focus on the planning of these activities/programs. Because of the diversity of the leisure industry, a program or event could range from an organized walk to a concert or festival. Whatever is envisioned, there are patterns and procedures that should be followed to facilitate success, the most important of them being forethought, action, and follow-through.

An old trick is to use an outline to focus on the entire project and its requirements. The example presented here is a basic generalized recipe intended to demonstrate the breadth of planning projects, events, and activities. Only you can determine exactly what is best for your organizational requirements. As always, the more planning that is involved, the less likely something is to go wrong. Consider the following questions and comments when planning your next activity or event:

I. **WHY**.   Asking why the activity is needed helps bring needs, intentions, and objectives into focus, and involves matching customer needs and the business' desires.

    A. *Selection of Goals*

        1. Raise money or labor for a cause (charity, benevolence), create business, create profits, generate awareness, satisfy clientele, meet social needs, etc.

II. **WHAT**.   Brings the picture into focus by beginning the structural process. This is when needs and ideas are joined and marks the start of the actual materialization of ideas. Sanction enough time for the entire planning, implementation, and completion process.

    A. *Identification of Program/Activity Possibilities (and Alternatives)*

        1. What is it you wish to do? What is it your customers exactly want? What do you hope to accomplish? Who will be your customers? How many customers are anticipated? How much money do you have? What will be your financial needs (including equip-

ment and labor)? Is it for profit/nonprofit? How many employees/volunteers are needed? What equipment is available?

2. Investigate long-term effects (for the business, community, environment).

B. *Determine the Methods Used to Obtain Objectives*

1. Will the activity(s) be music oriented/educationally oriented/competition oriented? Will they be participative? Will they be observational (e.g., theater, concert, lecture)?

C. *Selection of Possible Locations and Time Frames (and Alternatives)*

1. Is the location safe for customers? Will it contain the event and its participants? Does it provide necessary venues? Will you need authorizations, permits, licenses, etc.?

2. When is the best time to maximize participation? When will the event be held? Will it conflict with other popular activities/holidays?

D. *Selection of Managers/Leaders*

1. Who will head up the program(s) or activity?

III. **HOW.** Constitutes the *actual planning* of the activity/program/ event. The selection of what is to be offered has been made. *Do not assume anything* during this process.

A. *Accumulation of Resources*

1. Amount and type of people, money, equipment, materials, and facilities.

2. Insurance requirements investigated.

3. Legalities investigated. Liabilities known, waivers/ forms needed.

B. *Financing the Project* (Although placed here, financing is a concern throughout the entire planning process and requires constant reassessment.)

1. Full determination of costs and development of revenue providers (ticket sales, rentals, retail operations, food/drinks service. . . . Perhaps renting or contracting out various services.)

2. Allocation of financial resources.

C. *Distribution of Assignments* (Break up activity/event into manageable pieces [and put into writing].)

1. Research, selection, and appointment of the best person(s) for the job.

2. Research and selection of outside people, caterers, vendors, contractors, etc.

3. Making appropriate compromises when necessary.

4. Addressing safety concerns/needs (continuous)
   a. first aid kits
   b. qualified staff/safety checks
   c. paramedics on site?
   d. police notified

5. Plan the clean-up operation.

D. *Communication* (an ongoing activity from the beginning)

1. Establishment of communication pathways for all involved parties.

2. Advertisement (marketing). How will you "get the word out" (e.g., invitations, newspaper ads, radio, flyers, posters, etc.)?

E. *Trial Runs or Final Preparations*

1. Ensure everyone knows of their duties/responsibilities/contingency plans.

2. Fix/adjust any current problems/foreseen problems.

IV. **WHEN**. The actual running of the event.

A. Be attentive as to what is going on. Again, do not assume anything.

    B. Expect the unexpected (do not ask why something happened, but instead, how to correct it). Remain calm, polite, and cheerful.

    C. Allow for flexibility/compromises.

V. **AFTER**. Everyone can be a starter, but how many can say they are finishers?

    A. Full cleanup.

    B. Evaluation/lessons learned.

    C. Expressions of thanks. Rewarding of congratulations.

Following through with ideas separates individuals who succeed from those who do not. Ironically, good ideas are often accepted as such only to be put away for later use and end up being forgotten. Procrastination is anathema to planning and is almost always a result of insecurity. Self-doubt and momentary lapses of confidence are normal emotions whenever an idea is turned into a new project challenge. Experience, education, and knowledge help to offset these insecurities and are accumulated over time. There are, however, other factors of equal importance that are under everyone's immediate and direct control. Remember the major case study exploring Recreation Services in Saudi Arabia? No one at the time held the dizzying array of postgraduate degrees and years of diverse experience that our predecessors had, and yet far more was accomplished. What enabled success was an overwhelming desire to do better, the humility to ask for advice, an enormous amount of persistence and integrity, and a good sense of fairness and prudence. Success was achieved by capitalizing on these omnipotent factors.

Throughout the planning of projects, activities, and events, there are a number of steps that can ease the action process by helping to instill confidence:

- Observe, ask questions, seek information and/or help.
- Learn to organize and prioritize.
- Follow through with ideas and solutions in increments of progress.
- Be action oriented, but do not ignore research/advice and avoid "analysis leading to paralysis."

- Be persistent.
- Realize that you (and others) will make mistakes; learn from them.
- Set an example of integrity for others.
- Make the most of what you have, and do not dwell on what you have not yet acquired.
- Maintain open communications with your co-workers and customers.

By planning new activities or events, we face difficult or new challenges that may appear frightening or seem insurmountable. Yet this is how professional growth occurs. Focusing on established goals and persistently following through with them in increments of progress enables problems to be overcome. Within every leisure professional lies a history of accomplishments that can be directed toward future projects, activities, and events. By choosing not to go it alone (in essence, teamwork), future possibilities are greatly expanded. Ultimately what we are comprised of as individuals and how we decide to develop and use these intrinsic qualities will determine the outcome for both ourselves and our leisure programs.

PART IV:
PATHS AND DIRECTIONS

Where to Go for Further Information

Change occurs on a daily basis, and it is important to stay abreast of new developments, studies, and goings on. Whether it be business transformation, management, or recreation information that is sought, the best sources to approach to obtain further knowledge are: your local library, colleges and universities with leisure programs, and leisure-based professional organizations. Most libraries have a section devoted to leisure and recreation, as well as one for various business and management-oriented material. The titles used in this book's bibliography are a good start.

As computers become more prevalent in smaller organizations, including libraries, subject matter can be found more readily with computer databases. If you are having trouble finding a particular subject, think of different word and phrase combinations that could be used to represent the subject. For example, "organizing a festival" may be found under "special events," "program planning," "recreation programming," or other combinations. Some libraries even have an Internet service available to members.

Searches on the Internet, regardless of the country (Denmark has more Internet users per capita than the United States), are conducted much the same way. Key words such as "leisure," "recreation," "hobbies," "sports," etc., are used to initiate a search. Coupled with the words "management," "idea creation," "economics," "special events," etc., the search becomes more focused. Many public libraries have Internet stations where this search can be practiced. Because public libraries have qualified people dedicated to helping in the search for information, it may be best to begin there. Someone can almost certainly help to point you in the right direction.

Recently I walked into a small local library and the librarians were able to use their computer to contact the Library of Congress to check if a thirteen-year-old book filled with information and addresses had been updated. When it was found not to have been, they left a message and an e-mail address to inquire if another publisher had produced something similar and more recently. None was found, but someone did suggest an alternative. One of the best sources to find names of organizations and associations is *The Encyclopedia of Associations*, edited by Sandra Jaszczak and published by Gale. This encyclopedia is a guide to over 23,000 national and international organizations and can be found in most libraries; it is periodically updated.

Professional organizations are another rich source of information and material. Many are broad-based and fully cover the national or international specialty fields they serve. Through professional organizations, it is possible to narrow your focus down to smaller areas of the leisure profession that pertain to your interest. Smaller clubs and associations, with expertise and talents in specific concerns, can be contacted with the help of the larger organizations. When a commercial recreation business wanted to host a large special event involving customers and their bicycles, they were able to contact a nationally established bicycle club, with the help of one of the large leisure associations, that provided the information and know-how needed to establish a smooth-running operation. The club also presented the names of companies that specialized in insuring these types of functions.

Most professional organizations publish monthly or bimonthly journals (some posting job vacancies), disseminate ideas and pertinent leisure information, sponsor professional seminars, conventions, or symposiums, promote member involvement and interaction, provide lists of leisure books and publications (usually at a discount) as well as names of specialized manufacturers and suppliers, help with further education (some offer degree courses) and management or self-help issues, and, in general, further the cause and prosperity of the leisure industry.

Why not contact one or more of the following organizations to obtain further information? Space limitations prevent listing anything more than the most prominent. Remember that these organizations offer much more than what can be mentioned here and that addresses and offerings do change.

THE UNITED STATES

The National Recreation and Parks Association, 22377 Belmont Ridge Road, Ashburn, Virginia 20148.

The NRPA is an amalgamation of several agencies working together to promote unity, education, and professionalism in the leisure industry (each with its own information base). These agencies are:

- The Armed Forces Recreation Society,
- The American Park and Recreation Society,
- The Citizen Board Member,
- The National Society for Park Resources,
- The Student Recreation and Park Society,
- The National Therapeutic Recreation Society, and
- The Society of Park and Recreation Educators.

The NRPA publishes a monthly magazine, *Parks and Recreation,* which is full of relevant leisure information. It also publishes separate job and internship vacancy listings. The NRPA is involved with government lobbying and other issues that affect national parks and community recreation interests and concerns. There are a number of suborganizations focusing on aquatics, leisure concerns for the handicapped, fitness, park administration, and so on. Diverse information is available containing, among other things, college or university departments specializing in various leisure-related degrees.

The American Alliance for Health, Physical Education, Recreation and Dance, 1900 Association Drive, Reston, Virginia 22091.

The AAPERD is very education oriented and concerns itself with many academic issues including teaching and research. It is comprised of the following agencies:

- The American Association for Leisure and Recreation
- The American School and Community Safety Association
- The Association for Research Administration, Professional Councils, and Societies

- The Association for the Advancement of Health Education
- The National Association of Girls and Women in Sport
- The National Association for Sport and Physical Education
- The National Dance Association

Publications devoted to these areas offer subscriptions containing related information. Job positions (mostly teaching) are included.

The National Employee Services and Recreation Association, 2211 York Road, Suite 207, Oak Brook Illinois 60521-2371.

This specialty organization has been established for individuals employed in or involved with leisure programs within business, government agencies, and industry. For example, private parks, corporate fitness centers, company play/sport facilities, etc. The Association publishes *Employee Services Management* magazine, as well as fact-filled newsletters and information sheets providing program ideas.

The Resort and Commercial Recreation Association, P.O. Box 1998, Tarpon Springs, Florida 34688-1998.

As its name suggest, the RCRA is devoted to hotel, resort, and commercial recreation departments and businesses. This organization is very helpful. It promotes member networking and publishes *Resort and Commercial Recreation* every two months. Similar to many leisure publications, this magazine contains much information on matters for and about its specialty area, including listings of manufacturers and services established to provide the specialized needs and equipment of these areas. The Association also hosts numerous conferences and seminars and has a job placement service.

The American Camping Association, 5000 State Road, 67 N. Martinsville, Indiana 46151-7902.

This association publishes the monthly *Camping Magazine* and distributes books, pamphlets, and current information regarding camping and similar activities.

CANADA

The Canadian Association for Health, Physical Education, and Recreation, 333 River Road, Vanier (Ottawa), Ontario KIL 8B9.

CAHPER has been described much like AAHPERD listed above. Among the Association's goals, as described in the brochure, are: To participate actively in the establishment and the improvement of standards of practice of all who are entrusted with the responsibility of leadership in the field of physical activity, and to cooperate with any and all local, provincial, national, and international organizations that are committed to the improvement of the well-being of mankind.

GREAT BRITAIN AND IRELAND

Fitness Industry Association (FIA), Argent House, 103 Frimley Road, Camberley, Surrey GU15 2PP.

Many of my colleagues strongly attest to the excellent service, materials, and professionalism of the FIA. The organization exists to strive toward higher standards within the industry as well as increasing professionalism and a better marketplace for fitness. Training and development programs are available to members, businesses, and suppliers so that they may increase their skills and knowledge. The FIA also sponsors "Leisure Industry Week," the largest fitness-oriented exhibition and conference in Europe. FIA publishes three industry journals: *Health Club Management, Leisure Management,* and *Leisure Opportunities,* which is probably the most widely read leisure employment publication in the United Kingdom.

The Institute of Leisure and Amenity Management, Lower Basildon, Reading, Berkshire RG8 9NE.

ILAM is probably the premier leisure organization in the United Kingdom. This top-notch organization covers almost every conceivable area of leisure throughout England, Scotland, and Northern Ireland and even has a branch office in the Republic of Ireland. It offers respected degree and certification courses in the leisure field. *The Leisure Manager* is published bimonthly and contains current information regarding trends in the leisure profession, relevant issues and concerns, ideas, book reviews, manufacturers and suppliers, etc. A number of "fact sheets" are available containing brief yet highly condensed ranges of information on a wide variety of subjects. ILAM also publishes job listings, holds conferences, conventions, and seminars, and promotes leisure at a government level.

The Institute of Sport and Recreation Management, Gifford House, 36-38 Sherrard Street, Melton Mowbry LE13 1XJ.

This institute provides many training and education opportunities through a wide variety of colleges and universities throughout the Untied Kingdom. They also publish a magazine entitled *Recreation*. Training courses available through the organization provide certificates upon completion. In addition, the ISRM provides numerous industry-related publications, conference and exhibition information, and related advice and consulting.

INTERNATIONAL

The World Leisure and Recreation Association, 3 Canyon Road West, Let Bridge, Alberta T1K 6V1, Canada.

The Association publishes newsletters and a quarterly (themed) journal. Topics discussed involve a wide variety of interests and concerns, ranging from education to management issues. This international organization promotes interaction and communication between countries regarding the leisure field and industry, increases leisure awareness around the globe, and promotes research and education in leisure and recreation. They also host conventions that are held at many interesting locations around the world.

Conclusion

Networking and obtaining information are vital to business success, especially when that success is contingent upon change. For many of us, change must be faced anew, as if the wheel was being reinvented. In these situations, it is often possible to find someone who has experienced similar challenges and to learn from him or her. That is generally the point behind these associations.

When Michael B. was named as the new Recreation Director of a country club type leisure business, he had little or no experience in golf course operations. Ironically, the business he was to lead was constructing a golf course. Michael contacted several golf organizations and associations and became discouraged. To his astonishment, none seemed to be able to answer simple, basic questions about actual golfing business operations (many merely promoted the sport). Fortunately, his national leisure and recreation association provided the names and telephone numbers of member colleagues in the golf business. After a few telephone calls, he acquired the answers and solutions for which he was looking. All it took was a little digging and persistence (and talking with people who had actual hands-on, day-to-day golfing experience).

Business operations are a lot like that. It does not take a rocket scientist to come up with solutions. What is needed is an honest desire to improve, a bit of courage, an ability to work with others and seek out their opinions and solutions, the forethought to think ahead, and the commitment and consistency to *follow through* with ideas and suggestions. It is not always easy, but it is obtainable, and the results are well worth the effort, especially when they reflect favorably upon you and your organization. Success in leisure business is not contingent upon magic solutions or miracles. It is not achieved through shortcuts, gimmicks, trendy time-savers, or quick fixes. Success is obtained, pure and simple, by way of hard work intelligently applied and followed through until completion. This takes time and effort, and there is absolutely no way around it. Good luck in all your business endeavors as you strive toward improvement and success.

Bibliography

Administration of Leisure and Recreation Services. (1992). Croner Publications Ltd., London.

Armstrong, M. (1990). *How to Be an Even Better Manager.* Kogan Page, London.

Band, W.A. (1991). *Creating Value for Customers.* John Wiley & Sons, New York.

Barry, T. (1991). *Management Excellence Through Quality.* ASQC Press.

Brown, M.T. (1991). *Working Ethics.* Jossey Bass Publications.

Cole, G.A. (1993). *Management: Theory and Practice.* DP Publications, London.

Connors, T.D. (1993). *The Non-Profit Management Handbook.* John Wiley & Sons Inc., New York.

Cooper, C.P. (1989). *Progress in Tourism, Recreation and Hospitality Management.* Bellhaven Press.

The Daily Telegraph. (1990). *Guide to Working Abroad.* Kogan Page, London.

Davis, M.P. (1988). *The Effective Use of Advertising Media.* Hutchinson Press.

Deal, T. and Kennedy, A. (1988). *Corporate Cultures.* Penguin Books, New York.

Drucker, P.F. (1992). *Managing the Non-Profit Organization.* Butterworth-Heinemann Ltd., London.

Factsheet. (1996). Economic Statistics. Institute of Leisure and Amenity Management. Berkshire, England.

Farnsworth, T. (1990). *Fast Track.* Hodder and Stoughton.

Financial Report 1993, Employee Social Club. Finance and Accounting Services. Riyadh, KSA.

Financial Report 1994, Employee Social Club. Finance and Accounting Services. Riyadh, KSA.

Gabarro, J.J. (1992). *Managing People and Organizations.* Harvard Business School Publications, Massachusetts.

Gummesson, E. (1991). *Qualitative Methods Management Research.* Sage Publications.

Handy, C. (1993). *Understanding the Organization.* Penguin Books Ltd., London.

Harden, J. and Kauffman, R. (1996). "Something Old, Something New." *Parks and Recreation.* Vol. 31, No. 10, October, pp. 88-95.

Harrison, R. (1972). "How to Describe Your Organization." *Harvard Business Review.* (September-October).

Hingston, P. (1979). *The Greatest Little Business Book.* Hingston, London.

Hobday, P. (1979). *Saudi Arabia Today.* Macmillan Press Ltd.

Hutchins, D. (1992). *Achieve Total Quality.* Fitzwilliam Publishing Ltd.

ILAM. (1997). "Leisure is Key To Quality of Life. . . ." *The Leisure Manager Bulletin,* May, p. 1.

Jaszczak, S. (1996). *Encyclopedia of Associations* (thirty-first edition). Gale Research Company.

Jensen, C.R. and Naylor, J.H. (1990). *Opportunities in Recreation and Leisure Careers.* VGM Career Horizons, London.

Jordan, D.J. and DeGraaf, D.G. (1996). "The Dilemma of Sensitive Decisions." *Parks and Recreation.* Vol. 31, No. 11, November, pp. 54-59.

Joseph, R. and Ritchie, C. (1990). *Careers in the Catering, Travel, and Leisure Industries.* Kogan-Page Publishing, London.

Kantor, R.M. (1989). *When Giants Learn to Dance.* Simon & Schuster, New York.

Kindler, H. (1988). *Managing Disagreement Constructively.* Kogan-Page Publishing, London.

Koch, R. (1995). *The Financial Times Guide to Strategy.* Pitman Publishing.

Lacey, R. (1981). *The Kingdom.* Hutchinson and Company.

Lewin, K. (1951). *Field Theory in Social Science: Selected Theoretical Papers.* Harper Press, New York.

Mackey, S. (1987). *The Saudis.* Houghton Mifflin Company.

Majaro, S. (1988). *The Creative Gap.* Longman.

Maul, L. and Mayfield, D. (1990). *The Entrepreneurs Roadmap.* Saxtons River Publication.

McCalman, J. and Paton, R. (1992). *Change Management.* Paul Chapman Publishing Ltd.

McGee, R. (1992). *Business Ethics and Common Sense.* Quorom Books.

McGregor, J. and Nydell, M. (1981). *How to Live and Work in Saudi Arabia.* International Press.

Mercer, D. (1992). *Marketing.* Blackwell Business.

Minor, J.B. (1971). *Management Theory.* Macmillan Company.

Mintzberg, H. (1994). *The Rise and Fall of Strategic Planning.* Prentice Hall International Ltd., New Jersey.

Moore, N. (1987). *How to Do Research.* Library Association Publishing Ltd., London.

Mullins, L.J. (1992). *Hospitality Management.* Pitman Press.

Oakland, J. (1993). *Total Quality Management.* Butterworth-Heinemann, New York.

Pascale, R. (1991). *Managing on the Edge.* Penguin Books, New York.

Pearson, G. (1992). *The Competitive Organization.* McGraw-Hill.

Peters, T. (1988). *Thriving on Chaos.* Macmillan Press.

Porter, M. (1987). "Corporate Strategy. . . ." *The Economist,* 303:7499, May 23, pp. 17-22.

Postgraduate Prospectus. (1997). Glasgow Caledonian University, Glasgow.

Powers, C. and Short, C. (1996). "Survey Says. . . ." *Resort and Commercial Recreation.* March/April, p. 13.

Preece, R. (1994). *Starting Research.* Printer Publishers.

Pyle, R., Hall, J., and Whitehead, I. (1995). Letters and correspondence (October-December).

Sasson, J.P. (1992). *Princess.* Transworld Publishers.

Schein, E.H. (1969). *Process Consultation, Its Role in Organizational Development.* Addison Wesley Press.

Sisk, H. (1981). *Management and Organization.* S-W Publishing Company.

Solomon, R.C. (1992). *Ethics and Excellence.* Oxford University Press, Oxford, England.

Stamborski, J. (1997). "Ending the Perception of Article Elitism." *Parks and Recreation.* Vol. 31, No. 10, October, pp. 60-66.

Stewart, T. (1994). "How to Manage Change." *Fortune.* November 28, pp. 22-29.

Strebel, P. (1996). "Choosing the Right Change Path." *The Financial Times,* Part 14, February 9, pp. 5-7.

Stynes, D. (1995). *Leisure: The New Center of the Economy.* Denton, Texas: Academy of Leisure Sciences. (as quoted by: Godby, G. and Robinson, J. (1997). "The Increasing Prospects For Leisure." *Parks and Recreation.* Vol. 32, No. 6, June 1997, pp. 75-82.

Vail, P.B. (1991). *Managing as a Performing Art.* Jossey-Bass Publishers.

Vinnicombe, S. (1988). *Working in Organizations.* Penguin Books, New York.

Wasserman, S.R. (1983). *Recreation and Outdoor Life Directory.* Gale Research Company.

Watson, C.E. (1991). *Managing with Integrity.* Praeger Publishers.

Wilson, J. (1988). *Politics and Leisure.* Unwin Hyman.

Wright, J. (1989). *Recreation & Leisure: City and Guilds Course 481.* Croner Publications Ltd., London.

Ziglar, Z. (1986). *Top Performance.* Fleming H. Revell Company, New Jersey.

Index

Page numbers followed by the letter "i" indicate illustrations.

Abdul Wahhab, 12
Accountants, and finance, 131-135
Acquisition of volunteers, 126-127
Activities
  developing, 41
  planning, 163-168
Adapting. *See* Change
Advertising
  promotion, 138-139
  use of to acquire volunteers, 126
Al-Sawwa, Mujahid, 14
Amenities Centre, 72
American Alliance for Health,
    Physical Education,
    Recreation, and Dance,
    The (AAPERD), 175
American Camping Association,
    The, 174
Annual Financial Reports (The
    Club), 89-93,90i,91i,92i
AstroTurf, 76,77
Attention to customers, immediate,
  106
Attitudes, changing, 72-73
Audit, 133
Azziz, Abdul, 11,12,13

Badge policy, 38
Balance sheet, 133
Band, W.A., 56
Barry, T., 46
Behavior, changing, 85
Benefit perception, 143

"Best fit" theory, 68,69
"Blazing" memos, 75
Bottom line, importance of, 135
Breakdown pricing, 152i
Brooks, Graham, 107
Bundling, 152i
Business
  control of, 42
  efficiency of, 132
  flatter, becoming, 46,47
"Buzzwords," 87

Camping Magazine, 174
Canada, obtaining information
  in, 175
Canadian Association for Health,
    Physical Education, and
    Recreation, The (CAPHER),
    175
Captive pricing, 153i
Case study
  conclusions, 95-97
  The Hospital, 17-19
  introduction to, 11-27
  results of, 89-93
Censorship, 14
Chain of command pyramid,
  115i,116
Change, *ix,x,*33-35,83-84,145.
    See also Annual Financial
    Reports (The Club);
    Transformation
  commitment to, 33-35
  and constructive conflict, 67-68

Change *(continued)*
  and grounded, getting, 70
  initiating, 95
  introspect, 83-84
Change agents, 86-87
Change levers, 88
Change stage, 85
Change-force intensity, 86
Changing attitudes, 72-73
Changing behavior, 85
Cleaning of facilities, 40
Club, The, 19-26. *See also*
    Recreation Services
  Annual Financial Reports,
    89-93,90i,91i,92i
Cole, Gerald, 83-84
Commitment, 159
Committees, 144
Communication, 39,96
  interdepartmental, 46
Community groups, use of to acquire
    volunteers, 126-127
Compatibility, and pricing, 151-152
Competence, 34
Competition, sales, 144
Competitors, and pricing, 151
Complete system, 122
Computer, and obtaining
    information, 171
Confidence, 167-168
Conflict, 96
  constructive, 67-68,123
  dysfunctional, 123
  functional, 96
  management role in, 96
Construction, 40-41
Constructive conflict, 67-68,123
Control
  of business, 42
  fear of loss of, 33
Coolidge, Calvin, 59
Cooperation, 106-107
Costs, and pricing, 150
Courses, 145-147
Courts, sports, 73-74

Creating Value for Customers, 33-34
Creative variable pricing, 154i
Cress, Darla, 59
Culture, organization, 65-66
Current, recreation services, 99-100
Customer, 49
  complaints throughout renovation,
    80
  difficult, 109-113
  importance of, 107
  involvement, 137
  ownership, 144
  perceptions. *See* Process
  and pricing, 150-151
  volunteer as, 130
Customer interest, retaining, 142-147.
    See also Ten-session course
    plan, the
Customer involvement, 137,144
Customer loyalty, 130
Customer retention, 143-147
Customer service, 105-107. *See also*
    People, staff
  understanding good, 105-107

Daily Telegraph, The, 15
Davis, M.P., 52
Deal, Terrence, 65
Decentralization, 46,95
Decision making, and ethics, 158-159
Delegation, 121-123
Deming, W. Edwards, 160
Depth, 33
Development of new programs, 77-80
Differential pricing, 154
Differing segments pricing, 154i
Difficult customer, 109-113
Diplomatic Quarter, 79
Discipline, lack of, 132
Discount pricing, 153i
Driving forces, 84
Drucker, P.F., 60
Dysfunctional conflict, 123

Ecology, 62
Efficiency of business, 132
Empathy, 159
Employees, 39,87. *See also* Staff
    badge policy, 38
    and customer service, 106.
        See also Customer service
    expectations of, 117
    getting the most from, 115-119
    importance of, 106,115-119
    performance
        evaluation, 118-119
        rewarding good, 87
    specialties of, importance
        of balance between, 135
    termination of, 57-58
    training of, 106
Empowerment, 116,117,122
*Encyclopedia of Associations,
    The,* 172
Enlightened workplace, 116-117
Environment, 68
Equestrian program, 79
Equipment
    lack of, 23-24
    ordering needed, 40
Ethics, 157-161
    and customer service, 106,107
Evaluation of performance, 118-119
Event, planning, 163-168
Exchange, 62
Exclusivity (pricing), 153i
Executive Committee, 20-21
Exercise. *See* Gym; *individual sports*
Expectations of employees, 117

Facilities
    cleaning, 40
    construction of, 40-41
    renovation of, 40-41
Fairness, 158
Finance, 131-135
Financial control, lack of 132
Financial deal. *See* Promotions

Financial side, seeing only, 134
*Financial Times Guide to Strategy,
    The,* 21
Fitness Industry Association (FIA),
    175
Fixed pricing, 154
Flatter, business as, 46,47
Flexibility, 66,68
Follow through, 177
Force, 62
"Force-field theory," 84,85i
Foreign workers, 13,16-17
    recreational facilities for, 15-16
Four P's, 137
    place, location, 138
    price, value, 138
    product, service, 138
    promotion, advertising, 138-139
Freezing stage, 85
Friendships in workplace, 157
Functional conflict, 96
Functions, work-related, 49-50

Game room, off-site, 72
Gift-giving, 60
Golf, 78,143-144
Great Britain/Ireland, obtaining
        information in, 175-176
Grounded, getting, 70
Guests. *See also* Customer
    and pricing, 150-151
Guidelines for work, establishing,
        38-39
Gym, 74-76

Hall, J., 19
Handy, C., 18,69
    six style methods, 62
"Hard minds," 69-70
Harrison, Roger, 65
Heroes. *See* Leadership, strong
Hidden costs pricing, 154i
Hobday, P., 13
Hospital, The, 17-19
    Recreation Services and, 35

IMD (Institute of Management
     Development), 85
Individuals, use of to acquire
     volunteers, 127
Information, obtaining more
   in Canada, 175
   with computers, 171
   in Great Britain/Ireland, 175176
   international, 176
   on the Internet, 171
   at the library, 171-172
   in the United States, 173-174
*Institute of Leisure and Amenity
     Management, The,* 175-176
*Institute of Sport and Recreation
     Management, The,* 176
Interest of customer, 142-147
Intern, 129
International, obtaining information,
     176
Internet, 171
Involvement, customer, 137

Jaszczak, Samdra, 172
Journals, and obtaining information,
     172

Keeping volunteers, 127-129
Kennedy, Allen, 65
Kindler, H., 96
Koch, R., 21

Lacey, R., 12,14,18
Leader, 68
Leadership
   six style methods to influence, 62
   strong, 96
   style of, 59-63
Legality, 158
Leisure Manager, The, 176
Lewin, Kurt, 84
Liability, and volunteers, 125

Limitations, structural, 45
Location, place, 138
Long-term effects, 159
Loyalty, customer, 130

Mackey, S., 14,16
Magnetism, 62
Management
   and conflict, 96
   and employee relations, 117-119
   pyramid style, 18,115,115i,116
Management: Theory and Practice, 83
Managers, expectations from, 117-118
Marketing, importance of, 137-147
McGregor, J., 13,14
Meetings, monthly, 51
Memorandum, 27
Mercer, D., 51
Monthly meetings, 51
Mullins, L.J., 55,71
Mutowa, 16

*National Employee Services
     and Recreation Association,
     The,* 174
*National Recreation and Parks
     Association, The,* 173
Need for volunteers, 127
Networking, 177
Nonmanagers, expectations from, 118
Notice boards, 50
Nydell, M., 13,14

Oakland, J., 49
Off-site game rooms, 72
Operations. *See* Process
Organization cultures, 65-66
Outline for planning, 164-167
Outsiders. *See* Foreign workers
Ownership, customer feeling of, 144

Paralysis by analysis, 33
Participation, 142

Pascale, R.
  and shared values, 65,69
  and staff, 55
    skills of, 71
  and structure, 45
  and style, 59
  and systems, 49
  and transformation, 67,70,83
Pattern, 41
Pay as you go pricing, 152i
People, staff, 139
"People skills," 133-134
Performance
  evaluation, 118-119
  rewarding good, 87
Persistence, 168
Person culture, 66
Personnel. *See* Employees; Staff
Perspective, 41,159
Persuasion, 62
Physical environment, 139
Place, location, 138
Plan, 41
Planning, 42,125
Porter, M., 42
Position, 41
Power culture, 65-66
Powers, C., 105
Prevention, and difficult customers,
    112-113
Price, value, 138
Price performance, 154i
Pricing, 149-152
  types of, 152i-154i
Pride, 159
Procedures, 62
Process, 140-142
Product, service, 138
Product line, 154i
Productivity, 88
Professional organization, and
    information gathering, 172
Programs, developing new, 41,77-80
Project, planning, 163-168
Promotional pricing, 153i

Promotions, 138-139,144
Psychological pricing, 153i
Purpose, 159
Pyle, R., 19
Pyramid style of management,
    18,115,115i,116

Quality, 159-161
Questionnaire, effective, 137
"Quick action," scenario, 78

Rationalization, 42
Record keeping, usefulness
    of proper, 131
"Recreation Bulletin," 51,52,53
Recreation Services, 19
  and the Amenities Centre, 72
  and change levers, pulling of, 88
  and The Club, 19-26
  current, 99-100
  and decentralization, 46
  at The Hospital, 35,42-43
  improvement of, 31,32
  influence, methods used, 62-63
  problems at, 22-26,27i
  and shared values, 65-70
  staff, 55
    and skills of, 71-81
Recreational facilities, for foreign
    workers, 15-16
Renovation, 40-41
*Resort and Commercial Recreation
    Association, The,* 174
Responsibility, 159
Restraining forces, 84
Revenue, 21-22
Rinato, Romet, 56
Risk taking, 96-97
Riyadh. *See* Case study
Role culture, 66
Rules, 62

"Safe zone," 79
Safety, 23-24,37-38
  badge policy, 38
Sale, the, 142
Sales competitions, 144
Sasson, J.P., 15
Saudi Arabia. *See* Case study
Schein, Edgar, 85
Seasonal pricing, 152i
Sedona Health Spa, 105
Self-respect, 158
Serendipity, 87
Service
  cost of providing, 149
  as a product, 138
Seven S's, 81i
  shared values, 65-70
  skills, 71-81
  staff, 55-58
  strategy, 37-43
  structure, 45-47
  style, 59-63
  systems, 49-53
Shared values, 65-70
Short, C., 105
Six style methods, influencing
      leadership, 62
Skills
  lack of, 34
  of staff, 71-81
"Soft-hearted," 70
Specialized courses, 145-147
Sports courts, 73-74. *See also* Squash
      courts
Squash courts, 24,76. *See also* Sports
      courts
Staff, 55-58. *See also* Employees
  skills of, 71-81
Strategy, 37-43
  coordination of, 42
Strebel, Paul, 85-87
Structural limitations, 45
Structure, 45-47
Style, 59-63
Subordinates, 68

Surface covering, textured, 76-77
SWOT analysis (strengths,
      weaknesses, opportunities,
      threats), 42-43,42i
Systems, 49-53

Task, 68
Task culture, 66
Teams. *See* Teamwork
Teamwork, 95-96,121-123
Ten-session course plan, 145-147.
      See also Courses
Termination, of employees, 57-58
Textured surface coverings, 76-77
Thank you, 61,128
Top Performance, 115
Training, employee, 106
Transformation, 11. *See also* Change
  easing, 34-35
  fear of, 33-34
Transition, 34-35
Treatment of volunteers, 129-130
Trials pricing, 153i
Types of pricing, 152i-154i

Uncertainty, 33
Unemployed western wives, 51-52
Unfreezing stage, 85
United States, obtaining information
      in, 173-174
Usage, 141-142
User, 141
Uses, 140-141

Value, price, 138
Value-added pricing, 153i
Values, shared, 65-70
Vinnicombe, S., 18
Volunteers, 125,145
  acquiring, 126-127
  keeping, 127-129
  treatment of, 129-130

W. Edwards Deming Award
for Excellence, 160
Wahhibism, 12
Western wives, unemployed, 51-52
Whitehead, I., 19
Wives, western
unemployed, 51-52
Women, treatment of, 15

Work guidelines, establishing, 38-39
Workplace, enlightened, 116-117
Work-related functions, 49-50
*World Leisure and Recreation
Association, The,* 176

Ziglar, Zig, 115

Order Your Own Copy of
This Important Book for Your Personal Library!

FUNDAMENTALS OF LEISURE BUSINESS SUCCESS
A Manager's Guide to Achieving Success in the Leisure and Recreation Industry

_____ in hardbound at $39.95 (ISBN: 0-7890-0445-3)

COST OF BOOKS_____

OUTSIDE USA/CANADA/
MEXICO: ADD 20%_____

POSTAGE & HANDLING_____
*(US: $3.00 for first book & $1.25
for each additional book)
Outside US: $4.75 for first book
& $1.75 for each additional book)*

SUBTOTAL_____

IN CANADA: ADD 7% GST_____

STATE TAX_____
*(NY, OH & MN residents, please
add appropriate local sales tax)*

FINAL TOTAL_____
*(If paying in Canadian funds,
convert using the current
exchange rate. UNESCO
coupons welcome.)*

☐ **BILL ME LATER:** ($5 service charge will be added)
(Bill-me option is good on US/Canada/Mexico orders only;
not good to jobbers, wholesalers, or subscription agencies.)

☐ Check here if billing address is different from
shipping address and attach purchase order and
billing address information.

Signature_____

☐ **PAYMENT ENCLOSED:** $_____

☐ **PLEASE CHARGE TO MY CREDIT CARD.**

☐ Visa ☐ MasterCard ☐ AmEx ☐ Discover
☐ Diner's Club
Account #_____

Exp. Date_____

Signature_____

Prices in US dollars and subject to change without notice.

NAME_____

INSTITUTION_____

ADDRESS_____

CITY_____

STATE/ZIP_____

COUNTRY_____ COUNTY (NY residents only)_____

TEL_____ FAX_____

E-MAIL_____
May we use your e-mail address for confirmations and other types of information? ☐ Yes ☐ No

Order From Your Local Bookstore or Directly From
The Haworth Press, Inc.
10 Alice Street, Binghamton, New York 13904-1580 • USA
TELEPHONE: 1-800-HAWORTH (1-800-429-6784) / Outside US/Canada: (607) 722-5857
FAX: 1-800-895-0582 / Outside US/Canada: (607) 772-6362
E-mail: getinfo@haworthpressinc.com
PLEASE PHOTOCOPY THIS FORM FOR YOUR PERSONAL USE.

BOF96

FORTHCOMING and NEW BOOKS FROM
HAWORTH MARKETING RESOURCES

DEFINING YOUR MARKET `NEW!`

*Winning Strategies for High-Tech,
Industrial, and Service Firms*
Art Weinstein, PhD
Provides a practical and comprehensive base for defining and
redefining marketing in competitive and fast-changing global
markets. You'll find invaluable information about market
identification, analysis, selection, and strategy.
$39.95 hard. ISBN: 0-7890-0251-5.
$29.95 soft. ISBN: 0-7890-0252-3.
Available Fall 1998. Approx. 160 pp. with Index.
**Features case studies, tables/figures, review questions,
and appendixes.**

DEFECTIVE BOSSES `NEW!`

Working for the "Dysfunctional Dozen"
**Kerry Carson, PhD,
and Paula Phillips Carson, PhD**
A how-to, how-not-to, why, and why-not survival guide for
the journey into the inner workings of your defective
boss's world. The 12 personality types featured represent
the most common profiles of defective bosses.
$24.95 hard. ISBN: 0-7890-0580-8.
Available Fall 1998. Approx. 176 pp. with Index.
Features case studies and surveys.

GUIDEBOOK TO MANAGED CARE AND PRACTICE MANAGEMENT TERMINOLOGY `NEW!`

**Norman Winegar, LCSW, CEAP,
and L. Michelle Hayter, MSW**
You'll find the necessary information to understand the
terminology, jargon, and concepts needed for successful
practice and patient advocacy amidst the managed care
environment.
$39.95 hard. ISBN: 0-7890-0447-X.
Available Summer 1998. Approx. 113 pp. with Index.
Features appendixes and a list of organizations.

MEDICAL GROUP MANAGEMENT IN TURBULENT TIMES `NEW!`

*How Physician Leadership Can Optimize Health Plan,
Hospital, and Medical Group Performance*
Paul A. Sommers, PhD
Over 500 Pages!
Emphasis is placed on the role of administrators
in working as partners with practicing physicians
toward the provision of effective, accessible, affordable services
that provide high-quality health care.
$79.95 hard. ISBN: 0-7890-0487-9.
Available Summer 1998. Approx. 504 pp. with Index.
**Features recommended readings, tables/figures,
and a list of organizations.**

4X4 LEADERSHIP `NEW!` AND THE PURPOSE OF THE FIRM

H. H. Bradshaw
Over 200 Pages!
Learn how you can successfully move the levers
of change that will make the threefold dream of
increased trade, company and employee self-confidence,
and customer satisfaction a reality for you and your
company.
$49.95 hard. ISBN: 0-7890-0443-7.
$24.95 soft. ISBN: 0-7890-0444-5.
1998. Available now. 225 pp. with Index.
Features figures and interviews.

FUNDAMENTALS OF LEISURE BUSINESS SUCCESS `NEW!`

*A Manager's Guide to Achieving Success
in the Leisure and Recreation Industry*
Jonathan T. Scott, MBA
You'll have the benefit of 20 years of actual experience
in the leisure and recreation field at your disposal and
master the importance of contemporary business
management and techniques.
$39.95 hard. ISBN: 0-7890-0445-3.
Text price (5+ copies): $19.95.
Available Summer 1998. Approx. 200 pp. with Index.
**Features case studies, tables and figures, a glossary,
a list of organizations, and a bibliography.**

CONTEMPORARY SALES FORCE MANAGEMENT `NEW!`

Tony Carter, JD, MBA
Over 250 Pages!
Through the book's important discussions on lowering
mutual costs, building long-term customer relationships,
improving sales skills, and developing core process skills,
you will also learn to think and act with a strategic perspective
that successfully steers the sales process.
$49.95 hard. ISBN: 0-7890-0113-6.
$29.95 soft. ISBN: 0-7890-0423-2. 1997. 303 pp. with Index.
Features case studies and 41 charts/figures.

WRITING FOR MONEY IN MENTAL HEALTH `NEW!`

Douglas H. Ruben, PhD
Over 250 Pages!
The book's focus is on how to write stimulating
articles and book proposals, translate technical jargon into
plain English, and stay up to date with insider tips that will
help you supplement your paycheck in a time of shrinking
referrals, clients, and opportunities for income.
$49.95 hard. ISBN: 0-7890-0101-2.
$24.95 soft. ISBN: 0-7890-0240-X. 1997. 290 pp. with Index.

The Haworth Press, Inc.
10 Alice Street
Binghamton, New York 13904–1580 USA